Means of Awakening

Also by the Author

Culture, Power and Agency:
Gender in Indian Ethnography
Co-edited with Lina Fruzzetti (2006)

Secret Freedom in the City:
Women's Wage Work and Agency in Calcutta (2003)

MEANS OF AWAKENING

Gender, Politics and Practice in Rural India

Sirpa Tenhunen

Stree

Means of Awakening: Gender, Politics and Practice in Rural India
was first published in 2009 by STREE,
an imprint of Bhatkal and Sen,
16 Southern Avenue, Kolkata 700 026

ISBN 81-85604-97-5
978-81-85604-97-8

Rs 345.00

Design and typesetting by Krishna Gopal Das,
74T Sultan Alam Road, Kolkata 700033
and printed by Web Impressions (India) Pvt Ltd
34/2 Beadon St, Kolkata 700 006.

Published by Mandira Sen for STREE,
An imprint of Bhatkal and Sen,
16 Southern Avenue, Kolkata 700 026.

To my mother Kaarina Tenhunen,
whose strength and courage
I have always found inspirational.

Acknowledgements

I OWE MY deepest gratitude to the villagers of Janta as well as the people of adjacent villages who have graciously shared their world with me and made my fieldwork such memorable and pleasant experiences. I am especially grateful to my host family, Abhiram Kundu and his extended family. I chose Janta as my fieldwork site thanks to Lina Fruzzetti and Akos Östör who suggested that I should carry out my research in the same village where they had worked. I am most grateful for their advice and help.

I wish to thank Tarun Mitra who introduced me to the village as well as Kakali Das, Mandira Bhaduri, Subodh Ghar, Asima and Paresh Kundu, Dana Sugu and Samik Pal for their research assistance. I also wish to express my gratitude to Aditi Sen who helped arrange my immediate departure to Finland when my father passed away.

I thank Ilse Evertse for editing the language of the manuscript. I am also grateful to Stree for its editorial support and its anonymous reviewer for many valuable suggestions. I thank the Academy of Finland for funding the research. I have benefited from discussing my work at various seminars in Finland, India and the USA. I have specifically benefited greatly from discussions with and comments from Sylvia Vatuk, Patricia Jeffrey and Nita Kumar, as well as from the audiences of different seminars. I have also drawn from debates and interaction with the faculty and staff of the department of Social and Cultural Anthropology of the University of Helsinki, where I work in Finland, as well as the staff of the Centre for Social Research in

Kolkata to which I am affiliated.

Ajit Bagdi, Rahul Nandi and their families and I do not have words enough to express our gratitude to Dr Devi Shetty who saved the lives of these two villagers. I would like to thank my sisters, brother and their families who have provided me with much needed distraction from work, reminding me that there is more to life than research. Finally I want to thank Juha Laitalainen for his encouragement and support.

Contents

Introduction

THIS BOOK explores politics, culture, and everyday agency in a West Bengal village in India. The broad aim is to contribute to the understanding of political processes by relating the study of political domain to that of cultural practices. Consequently, the subject matter of this book revolves around the relationship between the active consciousness and the taken-for-granted form of consciousness: how social life entails reproduction, and yet change is often forged in homes and away from public debates, while personal experiences and everyday activities may also turn into politicized issues.

It was my encounter with the rural women of West Bengal, who are increasingly participating in politics, which brought me to delve into the process of consciousness building or 'the awakening' *(jagaron)* as the village women call it in Bengali, and this book presents a study of women's political participation and everyday practices in Janta, a village in the Bankura district of West Bengal. Historical records speak of rural women's mass participation in a broad range of political movements and survey-based studies, confirm women's increasing participation in politics in rural West Bengal (Kumar and Ghosh 1996; Sen Chaudhuri 1995). Yet anthropological studies on local politics in rural West Bengal and India (such as Nicholas 1966, 1998; Davis 1983; Bailey 1990; Lieten 1992; Ruud 2003) have either focused on men's political participation or noted women's non-attendance at political meetings in the villages.

The women of rural West Bengal have recently emerged at the forefront of the rural uprisings against the setting up of special economic zones in West Bengal. These rural protests resulted in the Tata company relocating its car factory from Singur in West Bengal to Gujarat. In 2007 the state was forced to reverse its plans of setting up a chemical hub in the villages of Nandigram in Midnapur district because of the farmers' resistance. The proposed special economic zone would have included fertile, irrigated land, and the farmers were not willing to trade their livelihood for a monetary compensation they considered meagre. Although the state had promised to respect villagers' opinions, it sent a police force to subdue the farmers' resistance. Police ended up firing at the villagers, killing fourteen and injuring many. Instead of exemplifying the benefits of the new economic policies, West Bengal turned into a showcase of the conflicts ensuing from economic liberalization. Land disputes have put the limits on the ability of political rulers to dictate local politics to a concrete test in rural West Bengal. This book helps one understand the nature of political processes and the relationship between the opposition and the CPI(M) rule in present-day rural West Bengal.

Rather than focusing merely on women's political activities, this book takes as its starting point the analysis of the cultural concept of politics in the village. In order to analyse consciousness building and the interconnections between different forms of agency, I examine how the domain of politics and perceptions of development relate to women's daily activities, alternative discourses, and subversive practices. Women's political participation in rural India is often associated with kinship in that female politicians are suspected of acting as mere proxies for the men in their families. I argue that the role of kinship in women's political participation is far more fundamental; it underlies both the local concept of politics as well as women's participation in politics. I will show how the local political domain is related to the cultural construction of gender and kinship and how this particular configuration of the concept of politics shapes political agency. Since the local concept of politics does not exclude home, kinship, and the women's domain, the gendered understanding of politics not only limits women's political participation, but also enables and shapes women's political action and critical discourses. I will show how the linkage between the cultural domains of politics and kinship makes parties efficient, while also making politics a vulnerable and conflict-ridden business that allows national party organizations to intervene and consolidate their power through family disputes. Political parties and women's organizations have been able successfully to involve rural women by applying the nationalistic ideas of women as the protectors of society, because this view resonates with the village understanding of the political.

This study is based on fifteen months' fieldwork in Janta in the Bankura district of the state of West Bengal: seven months during 1999-2000, four months in 2003-2004, and two months each in 2005 and 2007-2008. Concentrating on one village has enabled a nuanced understanding of the local meanings; however, my research also extends the village boundaries. I relate the village with wider ongoing changes and structures and examine villagers' connections outside the village. I also interviewed women political activists of the entire panchayat (elected local administrative organ covering sixteen adjacent villages). Throughout the book, I relate my observations to other studies on women's political participation in other parts of rural India. The focus is on the cultural aspect of politics, and my analytical approach is interpretative, although I also present quantitative data based on the household census of the village I collected. The bulk of the material consists of observations and taped interviews with seventy-six villagers, most of whom, sixty-seven, were women.

Janta is located 167 km northwest of Kolkata and by road 14 km north of the nearest administrative center, Vishnupur. Bordered by immense paddy fields, Janta, with its clustered houses, is densely populated by its 2,328 inhabitants (author's own census, 2004). Like its south-eastern neighbouring state, Midnapur, Bankura is well suited for agriculture, thanks to the alluvial soil and low-lying groundwater resources that its eastern neighbour, Purulia district, lacks. In contrast to some of the more industrialized eastern and northern districts of West Bengal, Bankura district relies predominantly on agriculture. Janta's main source of livelihood is paddy cultivation with most landowners also growing vegetables. Sixty-two per cent of the adult male population in Janta are farmers and 21 per cent labourers, most of whom periodically engage in agricultural labour (author's own survey in 2004).

In describing the social dynamics in the village, the book contributes to the debate on the Left Front government's role in respect of social change in rural West Bengal (Lieten 1992, Gazdar and Sengupta 1999; Mallick 1993; Basu 2001; and Bhattacharyya 1999), especially regarding gender relations. West Bengal has been governed and ruled by the Left Front and the largest left-wing party, the Communist Party of India, CPI(M), since 1977. Following the introduction of quotas for the lower castes and women by the Central Government in 1993, Janta's panchayat representatives have been women and low caste men.

In the 1990s, West Bengal witnessed the rise of the opposition which is formed by two parties: Trinamul (an opposition group that split from the Congress Party under the leadership of Mamata Banerjee) and the BJP (the right-wing Hindu Bharatiya Janata Party which ran the central government, 1999-2004). In the 2009 Parliamentary elections, Trinamul was allied to the Congress Party, helping Congress to win the election. During my visit in Janta, the Tilis, the largest caste group in the village, changed their affiliation from the Left Front to the BJP. Consequently, this book also portrays the rise of the opposition in the village.

The following few examples of political incidents illustrate how enmeshed politics, gender and kinship are in the village, while also highlighting the conceptual issues and questions at stake. One morning, during the first week of my fieldwork, everybody I came across seemed shocked. A man from the neighbourhood had been stabbed the night before and later died of his injuries. The women told me what had happened and mentioned that the stabbing was about *rajniti* (politics). The elder brother of my host family, however, remarked that the stabbing had occurred while two 'brothers' had been fighting over land. The victim and the murder suspect were cousins and the suspect's natal family was criticized for having received more than its legal share of the joint property.

I wanted to learn the truth about the murder and could not help but notice that the two explanations seemed irritatingly irreconcilable. As I learnt later, the stabbing was labelled political because it involved kinship ties of the local CPI(M) leader and activist. Both men supported the Left Front, and the victim's wife had been elected to the panchayat as the Left Front's representative. The suspect was accused of having stabbed his party and cousin 'brother'. The victim's family was devastated, whereas the rival political family saw an opportunity. The BJP held a public meeting in the village after which almost the entire Tili community in the neighbourhood changed its affiliation from the CPI(M) to the BJP.

Another political incident occurred when a Bagdi (low caste) villager, who was also a Communist Party supporter, made a dubious comment about me ('I wonder if her skin is soft'). I had no idea of the repercussions that this remark would have. The villagers regarded it as a serious insult and a threat to my honour. What made the situation especially critical was that I was living with a Tili (higher caste) family in a neighbourhood where people had newly switched from the CPI(M) to the BJP. The following day, the local BJP expressed its uneasiness about the situation and—ostensibly to protect me—forbade me to enter the Bagdi neighborhood.

Such incidents illustrate that the villagers do not understand politics as being separate from private homes, questions of honour, caste and kinship. My experiences are in line with the anthropological stream of the past few decades (such as Rosaldo and Lamphere 1974; Yanagisako 1974; Rogers 1975; Collier and Yanagisako 1987; and Strathern 1988), which illustrates the need to question the preconceived notions of power and politics as public phenomena. The pioneers of political anthropology, Evans-Pritchard (1940) and Fortes (1945), explicitly dichotomized the domestic domain to contrast with the politico-juridical domain. The same dichotomy is implicit in a later definition of politics as public, goal-oriented activity (Swartz et al. 1966 : 7 and Swartz 1969:1).

The notions of power and politics have been most radically expanded by the large body of scholarly works that, drawing from Foucault, emphasize cultural categories as negotiated and contested in everyday life. Instead of delving into the complexities and manifold nuances of these works, I merely want to point out that the propagation of all social life as political fields of power struggles leaves us unable to answer the following questions. Firstly, what is understood as 'political' in local settings? Secondly, to what extent does people's everyday agency draw on their understanding of power and politics? Thirdly, and more particularly, what should one make of the political conflicts in this West Bengal village where I conducted my fieldwork?

Works on the symbolic construction of politics, as those by Dumont (1970); Geertz (1980); Davis (1983); Östör (1984); and Kapferer (1988), have considerably broadened the understanding of politics by questioning the universal applicability of the Western domains of politics, religion, and the economy. Yet these stimulating works have paid little or no attention to the way the settings conventionally regarded as non-political, such as the home and the women's domain, relate to the political domain, and to how the conceptualization of politics as gendered contributes to women's role in politics.[1] Nor have scholars of rural India, who have long noted the importance of quarrels, rivalries, and disputes over honour, paid much attention to the implications of these events for the symbolic understanding and the gendered nature of politics. Unlike the academics, the villagers do not need lessons in the political nature of everyday life. Villagers share taken-for-granted ideas about the sphere of politics that cannot be grasped by classifying everyday forms of resistance as separate from conventional political activities, as Scott (1985) does, nor by concluding that all social activity is about power.

My approach to studying the implementation of political ideas in a village of West Bengal shares with Ruud (2003) the interest to look at how village polity is strongly influenced by the larger world and yet largely follows its own concerns. My study adds to the ethnography of West Bengal by looking at the cultural construction of politics and its relationship to the larger symbolic whole and especially gender. Drawing from Schneider (1980), I perceive culture as relating to social organization by presenting indigenous categories of social organization. My approach differs from that of Schneider in that I view culture as being in constant flux and also because my focus is on the reinterpretations of cultural categories in social interaction, on culture in motion, as discourses. Such symbolic fields as kinship and rituals represent dominant practices and enduring meaning structures, which cannot be ignored by the villagers; and nor can they be overlooked when interpreting village life. Nevertheless, these structures exist in motion, providing a basis for the generation of diverse and even conflicting positions and views. Consequently, my interest lies in looking at dominant practices, at the multiplicity enabled by symbolic structures as well as alternatives and inconsistencies.

In focusing not only on the concepts of power and politics, but also on their enactment, my study goes beyond those on the cultural construction of politics and power which have left the question of political agency open (such as Geertz 1980; Dumont 1970). My approach resembles studies that have addressed political practices in their cultural form, such as those by Davis (1983) and Hansen (1999), but it differs in that I do not proceed from a general definition of politics. Like Davis and Hansen, political scientists have tended to remain faithful to Cohen's pioneering formulation of politics and culture (1974), which relies on a separate conceptualization of politics and political culture;[2] despite the interest in examining political practices as a cultural phenomenon, politics is given a general definition.

This study aims to incorporate politics into the study of agency as cultural practices. The main concerns of practice theory were preceded by debates in political anthropology, especially by the action theorists (to name a few, Turner 1957; Bailey 1990; and Barth 1959). Yet the theories of practice and agency (Ortner 1984 and 1989; Bourdieu 1992; Sahlins 1987 [1985] and de Certeau 1984; Hekman 1995; Kumar 1994; Giddens 1994) tended to exclude the study of politics, although the understandings of power and politics form a crucial cultural arena for agency. The similarities between the questions posed by the action theorists and practice theorists are striking, although the former did not elaborate on their concept of culture or relate action to culture. Both Turner (1957) and Barth's focus (1959) was on the role of the individual in social processes, while the game metaphor led Bailey to discuss the structural constraints of action. Predating Giddens (1994), Bailey drew attention to the unanticipated consequences of actions. His view of politics as a game of honour resembles Bourdieu's definition of symbolic capital as the key intent of social action. Bailey's view of political action (1990: 87) was ground-breaking in that he emphasized the beating of the system more than its reproduction. However, Bailey does not make his concept of culture explicit, but chooses to work with the notions of norm, rule, and game; consequently, he takes the meanings of politics, religion and culture for granted.

THE STRUCTURE OF THE ARGUMENT

To sum up, I examine the symbolic bases of political action as well as the relationship between politics and other forms of agency. How is the sphere of politics understood and enacted? How does politics relate to other domains of agency? What consequences do the local understandings of politics have for women's agency and participation in politics? The focus is on gender, but in relation to the broader cultural and social whole as well as translocal relationships. I consequently proceed by outlining the social structure and the domain of politics before turning to women's activities. My focus on agency necessitates the examination of the diversity in the village, and each theme is examined from the gender, caste and class point of view.

Chapter 1 describes the setting of the research in the village as patterns of social interaction among villagers, between the village and the outside world as well as my position within the rural networks. Chapter 1 also describes the research materials I collected from the many networks. My fieldwork took place at the time when rural infrastructure improved considerably, thanks to the building of mobile phone networks in areas which till 2007 did not have a landline network. As these changes have a bearing on village politics as well as women's agency, I will explore the rural networks and their intensification as part of the research setting.

Chapter 2 examines recent social changes in the village in order to outline the major social divisions and changes as well as the villagers' perceptions of these changes. Villagers' views on development include discourses on personhood and relate to the local concept of politics, as revealed in Chapter 3, which focuses on the political domain. Chapter 2 further illustrates how development is perceived, practiced and put on display as a bodily process involving the essences of personhood (*khaua, makha, pora,* or, literally in English, eating, rubbing of oil and wearing of clothes) and is linked with other discourses on personhood: gender, caste, class, and kinship.

Chapter 3 describes the villagers' understanding of politics and how the rival parties deploy the concept of politics in an era in which state policies and new agricultural methods contribute to an increase in resources as well as in the dispersal of power in the village. The party organization in rural Bankura presents itself as a hierarchical system, much like a family, and the top level of the local party organization is expected to act as a patron to its followers. Political discourse in the village parallels that of kinship morality, and the political parties' demand for justice means that the parties are expected to act in keeping with kinship ideals. Changes in political affiliation and fissures among party members relate to serious insults and outright breaches of kinship solidarity between party members. Kinship forms the metaphor for the party and its activities, so that the relationship between kinship-based party members is differentiated from kin defined by blood relations, code of conduct, sentiment and spatial aspects.

Although political relatives resemble other types of relatives in a moral sense, there are also crucial differences. Party membership is, after all, less arbitrary than kinship: one cannot select new blood relatives or *kutum,* relatives through marriage, although one can easily change one's political affiliation. On the one hand, political kinship draws on the idioms of kinship, but does not equal other forms of kinship. On the other hand, kinship and party membership overlap, creating conflicting solidarities. It is the overlap between party membership and kinship that allows parties to be efficient, but also makes politics a vulnerable and conflict-ridden business.

Interpreting the local concept of politics points to the role of gender in politics. Gender in politics and women's political activities are the topics of Chapter 4 which illustrates how ideas of kinship underlie both the concept of politics and women's political participation. This chapter discusses women's political activities in Janta with the aim of understanding the cultural logic behind women's increasing political participation as well as their continued absence from some key political events. Culturally conceived, interrelated domains of kinship, gender, and politics do not merely limit women's political role and reduce them to proxies of the men of their families; they also enable and shape women's political action and critical discourses. Chapter 4 also discusses the impact of women's quotas on local governing organs (introduced in rural India in 1993), showing how the world's largest experiment with the decentralization of governance has indeed helped to overcome the problems of women's separate activism. Women still do not participate in the village general meetings, but through panchayat reforms they have gained entry to panchayat meetings and general village meetings called by the panchayat. Women's entry has not changed the concept of politics completely, but shown the fluidity of the cultural code of conduct for women. Since women's political activities in villages are supported by political institutions, parties and the state, this chapter also considers the articulation between these institutions and local discourses.

Chapter 5 examines women's perceptions of development, relating them to their daily activities, alternative discourses and subversive practices, illustrating that change occurs independent of discourses on change and modernity. Although less heterogeneous than urban areas, village society offers opportunities for alternative discourses and subversive practices such as family fights, love marriages, suicide threats and suicides, which, to a large degree, are not conceptualized as part of development, modernity, or politics. The overall aim of the chapter is to portray the multiplicity of agency and to examine how the different spheres of agency relate to one another. How does the local concept of politics (the topic of the preceding chapters) relate to women's other forms of agency and what is the relationship between women's personal goals and demands for broader changes in society?

Instead of radical changes, many women have experienced subtle reforms in family life, to which the increase in the general standard of living has contributed. Besides politics and the discourses on development and consciousness building, there is another realm of power struggle in the village: the business of ordinary family life with its disagreements and quarrels *(jhogra)*. Quarrels range from a scolding *(bakan deua)*, refusal to speak to someone *(kotha bole na)*, use of abusive language *(galagali)*, hitting, running away, threatening with suicide and even committing suicide. Chapter 5 also demonstrates love marriages as an example of how alternative meanings, such as the idea of romantic love, can travel from one social circle to a broader and a more public context. I illustrate how raising subversive ideas publicly, like going through with a love marriage, is not achieved through withdrawal or an escape from the dominant ideas and discourses, but rather by reinterpretations of the dominant structures of meaning.

The conclusion presents the summary of the ethnography and analysis, elaborating on the implications of the study for the understanding of power, politics and agency. The interest in practice and agency in anthropology has to a great degree excluded the sphere of politics as well as the actors' capabilities to directly criticize the status quo. The predominant view from which to analyse the domains of discourse, which draws from Marxist scholarship, has been to separate two forms of discourse: the active form of consciousness and the taken-for-granted forms of consciousness.

My study concurs with those that perceive all social life as contested in that I found no domain particularly static. Instead of the two domains of discourse–the active and the taken-for-granted forms of consciousness–I found several interconnected domains of discourse which derived their meaning from the symbolic system, none of which were free from contest of meanings. On the one hand, change takes place outside the realm of discourses on development and modernity; on the other hand, local interpretations of modernity and development are not complete departures from tradition.

Political concepts or the notions of modernity and development are not adopted because of their universality but because they are interpreted in terms of the local symbolic system, and can therefore serve as tools for moving the contest and questioning of meanings and ideals from small-scale contexts to broader ones. It is the connections and continuity between the local understandings of politics, discourses on development, and the myriad of subversive practices which allow personal issues and disputes, such as one's experiences of child marriage or family violence, to be applied to the discussion on how society should be changed. The notions of freedom, modernity, and development are not applied in local disputes because of their universality or the supremacy of the Western model of modernization, but because they offer concepts through which the taken-for-granted practices can be discussed and questioned. They are the means of awakening, of turning women's personal experiences into questions of social change debated in broad circles.

Notes

1 Östör (1984: 186) points out the need to examine and reconsider the preconceived Western relationship between politics and family. Davis (1983) includes an analysis of the incidents of family life in his analysis of political culture in a West Bengali village, but he proceeds from a general definition of politics as actions through which individuals, families, and castes aim to improve their rank in the hierarchical order. Kapferer (1988) elaborates on the parallel meanings of rituals and political riots in Sri Lanka, focusing more on the interpretation of rituals than on the actual riots, or on the rioters' motivations, interests, and perceptions of politics.

2 Cohen (1974: 36) defines political and symbolic realms as autonomous but interdependent. He proceeds from a general definition of economy and politics, thus overlooking the question of the symbolic construction of social domains.

ONE

Rural Networking

Going to Janta is a visually soothing trip along reddish dirt roads snaking between the shades of green of the lush paddy fields. The village is formed by clusters of densely built mud houses and cemented buildings, a few old temples and roofed meeting places *(atchalas)*. The housing materials indicate the village hierarchy: 74 per cent of the high caste houses and 26 per cent of the low caste houses are made of bricks and mortar (author's own census 2004). The brahmin neighbourhood–many of whose residents commute from the village to their government jobs in Vishnupur with its brick houses, boundary walls and gates resembles an urban area. In order to grasp the layout of the village and understand the logic of its social interaction, it is necessary to identify the various neighbourhoods by caste.

Table 1.1 Castes, Groups in Janta, 2004

Tili	1174	50%	Vaisnava	42	2%
Chasa	369	16%	Tamli	30	1%
Bagdi	340	15%	Cuta	28	1%
Napit	111	5%	Kulu	25	1%
Tati	67	3%	Akura	20	1%
Kumar	61	3%	Dhopa	10	0%
Brahmin	46	2%	Bihari	5	0%
				2328	100%

Source: Author's own survey, 2004

CASTE NEIGHBOURHOODS

The village is divided into caste-dominated neighbourhoods, with the exception of smaller caste groups who may live among other groups. Eleven of the twenty-three neighbourhoods of the village are strictly delineated by caste. Castes sharing the same neighbourhood–Tilis, Chasas, Tatis and Napits–are considered close to each other in the local hierarchy. Tilis regard themselves as higher than other castes of the village, except the brahmins and Vaishnavas. The lowest in the caste hierarchy are the Akuras and Bagdis, classified as Scheduled Castes by the government (see Table 1.1). The Tilis are the dominant caste in Janta, both in terms of numbers and as landowners, and I chose to stay among them.

Table 1.2 Men's Occupation in Janta, 2004.

	(Pop. over 18 years)	%
Farmer		
Land	440	55
Share	56	7
Labourer	164	21
Service	12	2
Business	28	4
Artisan	6	1
Priest	3	0
Barber	1	0
Student	73	9
Other	17	2
Total	798	

Source: Author's own survey, 2004.

The government classifies Bagdis, whose main source of livelihood in Janta is daily labour, as a Scheduled Caste. In Janta,

87 per cent Bagdis are landless whereas 59 per cent Tilis are landowners. Of the other castes, 50 percent own land. Some castes continue their hereditary occupations (Tatis are weavers, Kumars are potters, Napits are barbers and Cutas/Chhutars do carpentry), but with the exception of the carpenter caste, their hereditary occupations only supplement their income from farming (see Table 1.2). Most of the brahmins own land, but do not participate in farm work as other landowning villagers do. Most *paras* (neighbourhoods) have small grocery shops and tea stalls and there was a clothes shop owned by a Tili family. Grocery shops are run by the higher castes: brahmin, Tili and Tati families.

ADJUSTMENTS

I chose Janta as my field site after Lina Fruzzetti and Akos Östör, who had done fieldwork there and made an ethnographic film about it, *Seed and Earth*, suggested the idea. I do not use a pseudonym for the village, as it is generally known in the region that anthropologists have worked in Janta, and people from surrounding areas, for whom village identity would matter, would recognize the village even if referred to by a pseudonym.

I was introduced to the village in the blazing heat of May 1999 by Tarun Mitra, the retired head of the American Institute of Indian Studies in Calcutta, who knew the village. This introduction as well as the villagers' earlier encounters with researchers prepared them to view my arrival in practical terms. The Tili family, who had been informed of my arrival, was willing to assist me with my research and cook for me, but since they had eleven persons living in three small rooms, they were unable to put me up.

I rented a room in the village from another family. My new host family consisted of a widowed mother, her two sons and their families. The elder brother and his wife had a twelve-year-old son and six-year-old twin daughters. The younger brother had recently married. The family's newly-built cemented house, a square one with four rooms and a corridor running down the middle, had been build in anticipation of the eventual separation of the two brothers. The house had one entrance, but the space for the second door had already been prepared by plastering the spot for the door thinner than the rest of the wall. The sons' mother lived in one room, each brother had one room for his family, and I moved into the fourth room.

The villagers not only had an idea of what anthropological research work in the village entails, but also took it for granted that I would require a few special conveniences such as a covered place for bathing and a simple lavatory, although most villagers used the open spaces for both. Since I saw my role as one of adjusting to the local ways–which the locals apparently did not expect to the same extent–I would have hesitated to ask for these conveniences had they not taken these arrangements for granted.

Like countless village ethnographers before and no doubt after me, my initial experience of the village was marked by the shock of having no privacy. My room became such a popular attraction in the village that I felt I might as well have lived on the pavement. Spending time in other people's houses and on their verandas was far more peaceful than being in my own room. To my relief the tremendous interest in me gradually decreased, although I did have visitors daily throughout my stay. I genuinely enjoyed having a legitimate reason for spending my days having leisurely discussions with the villagers.

I presented the purpose of my work to the villagers by telling them that I would like to learn how village life and especially women's lives were changing and what the women's aspirations for change were. The women seemed to find this a relevant topic. It is difficult to assess in what way my identity as a Westerner influenced what the villagers wanted to discuss with me. They were eager to express their views on development, or, in other words, on modernities, but these discourses were no attempts to imitate Western modernities. For instance, when the young people spontaneously told me of their generation's new freedoms, such as the increasing popularity of love marriages, they made a point of noting how these new trends differed from Western lifestyles as perceived by them.

Despite the relative ease of my entry into the field, I stood out, not only because of the colour of my skin and hair, but as a single woman whose business was to roam around the village as much as possible, which was something an ideal Tili woman would not do. But I was able to negotiate solutions to the problematic situations. I could go anywhere at practically any time without raising suspicions as long as I was in the right company. During the day I was in the company of Asima, a married Tili woman and the wife of the eldest brother in her joint family. She assisted by accompanying and guiding me to the different neighbourhoods. Her husband accompanied us during dusk and nightfall, when it was not considered proper for women to move without a male companion. When I rented a car for errands outside Janta, it was not considered proper for me to travel alone with a male driver. At least one other man, or preferably Asima and her husband, accompanied me.

Thanks to the prior work of other anthropologists in the village, the villagers had an idea of what ethnographic fieldwork was about and they saw me as fearlessly dedicated to my work. Once, after we had returned to the village from a *mela* (a fair), the villagers told me that there was fighting at one end of the market area. They had purposefully chosen not to reveal this while we were in the market area because they anticipated that I would have insisted on observing the fight from as close as possible if I had known. Once when the police entered the village, a rumour was circulated about my wanting to have a chance to talk to the police. In reality the sight of the police car made me just as nervous as the rest of the village, and I had mentioned this to the villagers.

I would be readily invited—in fact, almost commanded to observe, photograph and videotape rituals. It helped that they realized I had come with a mission and had work to do, no matter what it was. They found it quite natural that I had ended up *(porechhi,* fallen) in Janta. (Women talked about the move from their natal village to their husband's as 'falling into' a certain village.) As a woman from a neighbouring house commented on my arrival in the village, a woman has to go where the duty 'falls'.

As with many other landowners in Janta, mobile irrigation pump sets that were introduced in the village in the early 1990s, allowed my host family to prosper in recent decades. Instead of relying solely on the monsoon rains, the movable irrigation pump sets allow the farmers to grow two or three crops of paddy per year, instead of the earlier single crop. The brothers had not only intensified paddy cultivation, but also sold the family vegetable fields near the house. This was a profitable, although unconventional, move: vegetable fields are called 'golden land', *sonar desh*, which signifies the high economic value of both the land and its produce. With the money obtained from the sale of the vegetable fields, they bought more land farther away at a time when it was still relatively cheap and, with the help of new irrigation technology, turned it into profitable farming land.

When her sons were young, the widowed mother supported the family by making puffed rice to be sold in the market. When I moved in, the family owned a brick house, a motorcycle and a jeep, which they hired out for weddings and to transport the sick to medical care outside the village. Having a westerner in the house, no doubt, added to their status, but unfortunately (for them) my work also required the type of mobility that went against the grain of behaviour befitting the family's new prosperity.

Before her marriage, the elder daughter-in-law had to walk to the nearest market to sell tobacco leaves and the sons' mother went to the market to sell the puffed rice she had prepared. Both women now cherished the fact that they did not need to go outdoors on work, although they still prepared puffed rice for sale, which was unusual for women of such a wealthy house. They were proud that their work no longer sent them away from home—an agent from Vishnupur arrived daily to take the puffed rice they had prepared to the market. However, their pride in being true housewives did not mean that they totally condemned women who stepped outside the house. On the contrary, they treasured outings: visits to other villages to see relatives and the cinema in Vishnupur. In fact, they often tried to persuade me to rent the car and take them for drives, which we did a few times.

Unlike most of the villagers, the men of my household did not see the nuances in women's outings, but simply wanted to confine women (including me) to the house. They said they considered me their little sister and felt they could not guarantee my safety, especially in the other village neighbourhoods. I often had the uncomfortable feeling that they would have liked to keep me as they did their pet bird—in a cage and fed generously. The brothers' attitude towards women who went out was considered unusually strict even within the village—one woman went so far as to tell the brothers that they suffered from an addiction to prohibitions *(baron korar nesa)*. Most villagers accepted the idea of women moving outside the home for special purposes: visiting relatives in other villages, going to Vishnupur on errands and to college. I never heard anyone disapproving of female health workers who cycled from village to village, female activists who travelled to meetings, or women who had office jobs.

The way in which I was able to carve a niche for my work in the village is telling of rural Bengal's social networks. I had made my initial visits to Janta from the nearby town of Vishnupur where I had been introduced to Habu Chowdhury, a wealthy, elderly merchant, a close friend of Lina Fruzzetti and Akos Östör. I was introduced to him as a student of Lina and Akos and he had told me that as long as he was alive, I would have no problems in the region and that he would look after me. I thought these words kind and welcoming, but thought no more of them until I began to understand how influential he was among the farmers. He dealt, among other things, in vegetables and had close trade links with the Janta farmers. When I learned that even the elder brother of my household had borrowed money from him, I requested my assistant to mention that Habu Chowdhury had offered to help me with my work, I no longer had to justify my moving about. On leaving Janta I discovered that the rest of what the old merchant had said about keeping an eye on me was also true. The agent from Vishnupur, who picked up the puffed rice prepared by the women of my host family, had regularly reported on my well-being to Habu Chowdhury.

EMERGING PATTERNS OF SOCIAL INTERACTION

The social networks of rural West Bengal, the most densely populated state of India (Census News 2001), have always been well knit. My fieldwork took place at a time when the rural infrastructure improved considerably thanks to the building of mobile phone networks in the region. As these changes have a bearing on village politics as well as women's agency, I will explore the rural networks and their intensification as part of the research setting. Local identity has always emerged in relation to broader networks—other villages, districts and cities through trade and kinship. Connections did not start with the use of information technology, although phones as well as radios and television sets have increased and intensified such links.

The nearest neighbouring villages are only a few kilometres away from Janta. Although the town of Vishnupur is only 5 km from Janta as the crow flies, the distance to the town from Janta by road is 14 km because the only bridge across the rivers—there are two rivers between Janta and Vishnupur—is further away from the village. There is a 6 km shortcut to Vishnupur but one has to cross the rivers on foot; which is possible only when the river lies low.

Nevertheless, the services of Vishnupur are available to the villagers. Most villagers take a bus or ride a bicycle to Vishnupur to go shopping or to see a doctor. There is no formally trained medical personnel in Janta except for a few men who learned nursing and medicine informally and practise in the village as doctors. Vishnupur, with its 61,943 inhabitants, is the administrative centre of the region as well as an educational town with three colleges. It has a large bazaar where farmers sell their produce and do their shopping, as well as markets for local handicrafts and imports from other regions of India. To travel anywhere in India or to many places in the region, villagers first have to go to Vishnupur's railway station or the bus depot. Despite its road connections the peaceful exterior of the village is rarely disturbed by engine sounds. There were four cars, five tractors, and several motorbikes during my fieldwork periods in the village.

Village exogamy (women usually marry outside their natal village) is responsible for most of the connections between villages. Before the building of the mobile phone networks, news of relatives in other villages, of women's natal families and men's in-laws, travelled via letters (among the literate part of the village) and visitors. Like most villages, Janta has a post office and a daily mail delivery. Visiting other villages also meant being informed of other people's news (*khobor neua*), and delivering it to the relevant people in other villages, often on request.

The visitors' networks, on which villagers had to rely for the news of their kin and friends in other villages and districts, were often slow and even unreliable. Women, for example, said that they often could not obtain the news of a serious illness or the death of a close relative in time to view the body before the cremation and to participate in the death rituals. The inadequate communication infrastructure together with the considerable measure of autonomy from state authorities and services that villages enjoy, contributed to the villagers' relative isolation. The more remote the village, the smaller the chances were of asking for or getting help from outside it in case of emergencies and conflicts.

Thanks to radios and television sets, which middle and large farmers started to purchase in the mid-1990s, villagers used to have a better access to world news than the news of their relatives in other villages. Radio and television have also successfully educated rural people about agricultural methods and public health issues. Movies, mainly popular Hindi and Bengali movies (in the past video tapes, but since 2000 DVDs), are shown daily in the village movie hall as well as in some of the wealthier houses.

By 2003, the village cinema hall was facing severe competition from a few television owners who had acquired DVD players and started showing movies for a small fee. Thanks to DVD players, movies can now be shown in all neighbourhoods. Films have consequently become more accessible to women because they no longer have to go far from their own houses to see films.

One of the village's most significant connections with the outside world is because of state policies: the village's main source of livelihood, agriculture, is heavily influenced by policies which draw from the global discourse on modernity and development, as Gupta (1998) illustrates. As most modern scholars of village India have been at pains to prove, Indian villages have never been the kind of static, self-sufficient communities described by the early British colonial observers, or by Maine and Marx.

However, even if villages were never isolated from the rest of the world, a village is a special kind of social unit. Villagers know one another and interact on a daily basis with many of their fellow villagers, especially in their neighbourhood, but also across caste lines. They identify themselves through their village and often draw from the idea of village sociability as a kind of self-sufficiency and self-rule.

INTENSIFICATION OF NETWORKS

In 1999-2000 most villages in West Bengal had neither electricity nor landline phones–at a time when urban India was already shifting toward the use of mobile phones and surfing the Internet. In 2002, the BSNL (a government-owned service provider) mobile phone network covered rural West Bengal and private service providers announced plans to open services in the region. Because the demand for BSNL connections exceeded the company's ability to provide cards, getting a BSNL card through the official routes required months. The first private company service provider, Airtel, which started its services in the region in 2004, made it possible to obtain a connection instantly.

In the fall of 2003, there were four cellular phones in Janta.

When I returned to the village in 2005, there were ten phones in Janta and its two small, adjacent villages. Phone services had become available for the entire village, thanks to BSNL which placed mobile phones for public use in all villages. As a fairly large village, Janta had received three public phones for its different neighbourhoods. These phones could be charged with the help of solar panels, making these functional even in areas without electricity. Public phones are operated by shopkeepers for a small profit. They are responsible for ensuring that the calls are taken and the concerned villager is informed when he receives a call. A three-minute call costs the caller Rs.2. Many phone keepers charge Rs.2 to deliver the news of an incoming call. People also use privately owned mobile phones for pay calls.

I filmed 100 phone calls in the public phone shops of Janta and two neighbouring villages (Subhaspalli and Dior) in order to find out how phones influence the patterns of social interaction in the villages. The majority of the callers were male (71 per cent) and the majority of the calls (58 per cent) were made to villages in the district: 12 per cent of the calls were to other districts, 16 per cent to other states and one call was made to the USA. Relatives received 81 per cent calls, 14 percent went to business associates and five per cent to friends. Table 1.3 gives a break-up of the call topics.

As Table 1.3 shows, most calls are about organizing a phone call. In the village, the ringing of a phone is the start of a long chain of messages. To talk to a person in another village, one first needs to alert this person to come to the phone, so the caller needs to rely on others to give this message to the relevant person in the village. Sometimes callers simply relate their message to whosoever has answered the phone, requesting this person to forward the message. A man who happened to be waiting for a call, for example, answered somebody else's call when the phone rang and agreed to deliver the caller's message—that the son did not want his father to take an agricultural loan from the co-operative bank because he was prepared to give the money—to his father. Those answering the phone also try to

Table 1.3 Topic of the Call

Organizing a call	31
Exchanging general news	31
Business	23
Visiting and travelling	17
Giving or receiving help	13
News about health	11
Organizing rituals	9
Marriage arrangements	8
School	4
Only arranging a call	26
Only business	17
Only general news	9
Only arranging rituals	4
Only marriage arrangements	3
Only help request	3
Only visiting	3
Only illness	1

Source: Author's own survey, 2004.

give as much information as possible on behalf of the person with whom the caller wants to talk if that person is absent. The shop owner, for example, told a caller that the person he wanted to speak to had left for Maharashtra. He searched for the man's relatives but since no one was present, he relied on further information given by the neighbours. When he realized that the call was coming from the vicinity of the railway station to which the man in question was allegedly heading, he told the caller that he suspected that the absentee recipient would probably show up at the caller's house and stay the night.

It was the public nature of the calls made that helped me research the use of phones: villagers are used to others listening to their calls. I explained my purpose to each caller and asked for permission to film the call. The public nature of most of the calls as well as the collective manner of operating the phones draws from village sociality and earlier patterns of communication in the village. Phones have not done away with the practice of delivering other people's news, allowing the villagers closer mutual interaction than before the arrival of phones when there were fewer messages to deliver. The difference is that the number of messages that have to be delivered has grown by several folds, and the villagers complain that phone owners do not deliver all the messages.

A great majority of phone calls are made between relatives, and the phones have thus strengthened the kinship system. These calls range from asking for help to casual conversation and the exchange of general news. Not all calls are about getting help in dire circumstances, but the villagers perceive the ability to call for help as one of the most crucial benefits of availing a phone service. After a severe hailstorm destroyed the farmers' spring crops, the villagers crowded the phone shops to inform their relatives of the disaster. Since the hailstorms did not hit the entire region, many were able to get help from relatives whose crops had not been destroyed.

Along with the kinship connections, the phones have also strengthened the region's ritual life. Instead of having to travel to invite each relative to a ritual, the villagers can now reach everyone by phone. Consequently, more relatives than before can attend rituals such as funerals and weddings, which are often arranged quite suddenly. Phones are also used to discuss marriage arrangements. People inform one another about arranged marriages, ask information about potential brides and grooms, ask advice about marriage offers and deliver news of the acceptance or rejection of marriage proposals. The most decisive part of the marriage arrangement is when the groom's party comes to see the potential bride. The girl and boy can see each other and afterwards give their opinion on the marriage proposal, although sometimes marriages are arranged without taking the bride's and groom's views into consideration. Phones help arrange these meetings and make it possible for the potential grooms to see more brides than they would before the arrival of the phones. Phones have also made it easier to express opinions on potential brides and grooms–rejections no longer need to be conveyed in person but by a phone call.

Although the majority of calls are made within kinship groups, phones serve to extend villagers' connections by helping to keep in touch with relatives who have emigrated to other districts or abroad. According to a woman whose son works outside West Bengal, they would talk to the son perhaps once a year before the arrival of the village phone, whereas now he calls his parents weekly. Moreover, the phones facilitate travel and visiting people: calls are made to find out about the concerned relative's whereabouts and set up meetings and visits. An increased contact with villagers who have moved away has resulted in more information on work opportunities outside the village.

Most phone calls do indeed take place within the neighbourhood, but the phones also make it possible to maintain rebellious and secret contacts. If villagers do not want their immediate neighbours and family to overhear the conversation, they commute to make calls from other neighbourhoods and villages. In case of disputes, phones make it possible to obtain support from a larger group of relatives and friends than before, and one can also keep in touch with fugitives from the law. In extending and multiplying villagers' relationships, phones are giving village society a multi-faceted character typical of urban settings. As this book will illustrate, an increased connection to the world outside the village may also contribute to changes to the village politics because the increase in connections outside the village lessens the dependence on local leaders.

Phones have clearly increased the communication between women and their natal families, although women form only a minority of the callers (29 per cent). All mobile phones in the village are owned by men, and so are the shops where one can access public phones. However, in many houses it is women who are in charge of delivering the news and operating the phone

Table 1.4. Call parties

To Whom	
Non-specified kin	25
Business associate	14
In-laws' house	13
Parents' house	12
Siblings	12
Uncle's house	5
Friend	5
Father's brother	2
Husband's brother	1

Source: Author's own survey, 2004.

because their husbands are out on work, purchasing stocks or selling products. As Table 1.4 shows, most of the calls are between in-laws.

It did not take the local entrepreneurs long to realize that mobile phones help extend one's clientele, and in my sample, business transactions represent a major call category. Thanks to mobile phones, micro entrepreneurs can now keep in touch with their customers, even when they are on the road or transporting goods. The farmers use the phones to obtain information on prices. Agricultural produce can now be sold on the phone. Previously, deals would be sealed by signing a written contact, well before the product was delivered. Sellers can now continue haggling with various buyers until it is time to deliver the products. The prices are negotiated over the phone at the very last moment, which has decreased the middlemen's profit and benefited farmers. One obvious economic benefit of phones is that that they help people to save time. One need not be absent from work and travel to meet people to stay connected. This is especially important for daily wage labourers for whom to miss a day of work may mean not being able to feed their family that day.

A chicken farmer was one of the first persons in the village to get a mobile phone. During that time he also purchased a three-wheeler. These investments increased his monthly sales from 30 quintals to 150 quintals. He soon bought a colour television and a DVD player. He was also the first villager to get cable television—he now has access to dozens of channels, including Western movie channels, the BBC, and several Indian movie channels, although most of these channels are not watched. I never saw anybody watching any channel other than the local Bengali and Hindi movie channels. His next investment was to buy the village's first refrigerator, which he used to store chicken.

My findings on the impact of phones in rural West Bengal show a peculiar duality. On the one hand, villagers from Janta mention having experienced the same benefits from phones, such as the ability to call for help, to save time and find market information, as do villagers in such diverse places as Tanzania, Egypt, South Africa, Bangladesh, urban India and Thailand (Bayes 1999; Loyola 2005; Coyle 2005; Bruns et al. 1996). In all of these places, phones are associated with a form of 'social logistics' characterized by the increased multiplicity of social contacts and market relationships' greater efficiency. On the other hand, in common with other ethnographies on the appropriation of ICTs (Miller and Slater 2000; Horst and Miller 2005), I have exemplified how the appropriation of phones draws from local culture. Phones in rural West Bengal have accentuated kinship ties and village solidarity.

As I have argued (Tenhunen 2008), phones amplify cultural patterns but do so selectively. This is possible because as Derne (2005: 46) puts it, all cultures recognize contradictory aspects of human experience, providing multiple cultural resources on which individuals can draw in times of change. Instead of travelling, visiting, and having long face-to-face discussions, phones reinforce the pattern of having brief conversations, non-face-to-face. As keeping in touch becomes more frequent and casual, the meanings of relationships change. The type of social interaction phones encourage depends on their number: as phone density increases, villagers share phones among smaller circles than before when there were just a few phones. Instead of supporting the power of village leaders, phones help to lessen their power by facilitating a multiplicity of relationships. Mobile technology has an impact on logistics, but not directly on cultural meanings because similar logistics can thrive in different cultures.

To sum up, the appropriation of phones in Janta has contributed to the intensification of kinship contacts and the invigoration of the local economy. As the following chapters will illustrate, phones were introduced in the region during an economically, socially and politically dynamic period. The improvements in communication infrastructure have accentuated these changes and communication networks that existed prior to the phones. The ability to stay in perpetual contact with one's relatives in other villages is changing the social setting to reflect urban society's multiplicity, although the way the phones are operated is also intensifying social interaction among villagers. It is this particular type of connectedness that gives village society its distinct features and which this study explores in discussing local politics and the efficiency of the broader organizations in the village.

RESEARCH MATERIALS

I visited the village a few times in May before settling down there in June 1999 and left the village at the end of March 2000. I spent a total of seven months there within the space of a year and was able to observe all the major seasons of the yearly cycle and the changes they brought to the rhythm of the village. Living in the village was a treasured and enjoyable experience. After returning to Finland, I have missed the village and found sitting alone in the office all day difficult, although I do also treasure my freedom of movement, my privacy, and not having to discuss my every move with the neighbourhood as I had to do when living in the village.

My return to Bankura for four more months of fieldwork in 2003 and 2004 and for two months in 2005 and 2007-2008 has helped me verify my findings as well as ascertain the direction of changes. On my return I opted to stay in Vishnupur from where I commuted to the village. It was easier to arrange a furnished room for a few months' stay on short notice in a tourist lodge in Vishnupur than in the village. I also appreciated such conveniences of life in Vishnupur as electricity and the bathroom after living in Janta where a snake once entered my bathing space, outside the house.

I was astonished at how easily, after initial worries about my safety, the villagers accepted my mode of travel: I commuted from Vishnupur to the village daily by bicycle. Cycling long distances was something they would not have allowed me to do when I lived in the village. Now that I was living outside the village, when people heard that I was commuting by bicycle, they commented, 'She has become local.' I felt that riding the bicycle indeed made me blend in. Cycling complemented my earlier fieldwork method of doing participant observation by staying in the village. I became familiar with many neighbourhoods and even the neighbouring villages of Janta by cycling through them daily. I also became acquainted with other people on the move: people riding their bikes, going in the same direction would often spend time riding next to me and talking to me. I also learnt to experience and understand the scope of the 6 km that separate the village from the town in the map. Pushing the bicycle in the heat through the rivers and especially the river sand is exhausting and entails more risks than just a heat stroke. Sudden hailstorms form fast and the hails are big enough to knock a person unconscious. Most of those who get regular work in Vishnupur prefer to rent a place in the town than spend two hours commuting on a bike or a bus daily. Cars and buses move at a snail's pace in the traffic jams of the narrow streets of Vishnupur. New bridges and roads are badly needed to bring more villages close to Vishnupur and its economic opportunities.

Since I lived in the village during the greater part of my fieldwork, I obtained much of my insights into village life through participant observation and chatting. The political incidents that I observed mostly occurred in the Tili neighbourhood where I lived. I also regularly visited other neighbourhoods. At one point the local BJP forbade me to visit the low caste neighbourhoods, but after I turned to the neighbourhood BJP leader for his permission, he gladly promised me his support and protection. After all, my submissive gesture reaffirmed his new position of authority in the village.

The focus of this book is on the cultural aspect of politics and my analytical approach is interpretative, although I also took a complete household census of the village. The census was carried out by three villagers whom I hired to do the work. The survey covers respondents' caste, neighbourhood, sex, age, marital age, occupation, education, caste, the number of children and the type of housing. Those villagers who have not had schooling often do not know their exact ages and could only conjecture. I left sensitive questions such as the size of the landholdings out of the census-related questions.

I carried out in-depth interviews with the local party leaders, four of whom belonged to the CPI(M)—the largest among the parties forming the ruling Left Front government in West Bengal—and four to the BJP (one Chasa, and three Tili men). Two CPI(M) activists I interviewed were low caste and two belonged to the Tili caste. I interviewed seven women who participated in political organizations: three had represented the village in the panchayat (village council) and the rest were active in the local women's committee. In addition, I had discussions with three women of the district-level organization of the women's committee and visited the CPI(M)'s local area office. The bulk of the material consists of taped interviews with seventy-six villagers, most (sixty-seven) of whom were women.

I carried out the taped interviews personally, in Bengali—I had a fair command of Bengali when I moved to the village, having worked in West Bengal earlier (Tenhunen 2003). Living in a village where only Bengali was spoken helped improve my Bengali and I also picked up the village dialect. I arrived at the number of villagers to be interviewed through an interpretative saturation process by moving to a new neighbourhood when interviews no longer elicited new information, or portrayed new cultural aspects. I use pseudonyms for most of the villagers I interviewed and promised confidentiality. However, I do not hide the identities of party representatives and activists who spoke to me as office holders. They are well known in the village and the region and would consequently be recognizable by their positions even if I had used pseudonyms.

TWO

Reform and Personhood: Development in Policy and Practice

The most significant recent change in Janta has been the acceleration of economic growth during the 1990s. This growth paralleled the unprecedented growth in agricultural output in the state of West Bengal from the 1980s onwards (Gazdar and Sengupta 1999). Both the small farmers and agricultural labourers of Janta describe the past decade's *unnoti* (development) as having brought an end to occasional food scarcity and hunger.

This chapter discusses the perceptions of development in relation to caste and class in Janta and analyses the social context of politics, political interests and motives in Janta. Since the impact of the Left Front reforms in West Bengal has spurred ample research on the subject (Kohli 1987; Lieten 1992; Gazdar and Sengupta 1999; Mallick 1993; Basu 2001; Bhattacharyya 1999; Bandyopadhyay 2003; Hill 2003), I start by relating the changes in Janta to this discussion.

The main reforms implemented by the Left Front include an increase in the redistribution of land held over the legal limit, the securing of sharecroppers' tenancy rights and the decentralizing of political processes by placing more power in the hands of panchayats, the village councils. The Left Front's 36-point programme also mentions general measures and goals, such as the right to work, the eradication of illiteracy, a social insurance scheme for the elderly, invalids, the disabled and handicapped, unemployment allowance, encouragement of the forming of cooperatives, and measures to help women fight and overcome their social and economic disabilities, as part of its aims. Many of the aims, which remain at the programmatic level in West Bengal as in the rest of the country, were also included in Indira Gandhi's 20-point programme.

Lieten's (1992) study on the impact of the Left Front reform in a village in the Birbhum district in West Bengal supports proponents of the Left Front government such as Kohli (1987) and the CPI(M) economist Biblab Dasgupta (1984). Lieten credits the Left Front with all the positive developments, not only in terms of land redistribution and decentralization of power, but also when it comes to advancements in literacy, health care, increase in agricultural workers' wages and the mental empowerment of the lower castes and women. He makes few intra-state comparisons and the ones he makes actually point to the fact that West Bengal's performance has not been that impressive. As various critics have pointed out, when compared with other states, West Bengal's achievements in education, health care and fighting poverty are average at best and often well below the national average. Indeed, most development indicators have not reflected a particularly laudable picture of Left Front reforms. Among the states of India, West Bengal has fallen from the fourth place (1971-72) to the fourteenth (1997-98) in terms of its infrastructure (roads, railways, ports, irrigation, electricity, telephones, loan deposit rates of banks and tax collection) (Banerjee et al. 2002). According to the Pratichi Education Report, West Bengal occupies the eighteenth position in terms of literacy. Only 42 per cent of the Scheduled Castes are literate, and the student teacher ratio is 54:1 (*EPW* 2002).

THE LIMITS OF THE LAND REFORM

Landless low caste workers' interests have not been a top priority for the Left Front. Despite thirty-two years of Left Front rule, West Bengal—much like the rest of rural India—still lacks effective regulation of the terms and conditions of agricultural employment (Rogaly, Harriss-White and Bose 1999:30). The agricultural labourers of West Bengal do not have their own union, but are jointly organized with landowners under the Krishak Sabha, the peasants' union, which is dominated by middle and rich peasants.

Janta's Krishak Sabha is led by a local CPI(M) leader, a wealthy peasant, who himself belongs to the Tili caste and together with his three brothers owns 20 bighas (1 bigha = 0.33 acre) of land. The top leader of the local CPI(M) party is one of the richest men in the village, but other wealthy peasants are also called leaders (*neta*).

The local brick workers' union differs from the agricultural labourers' organization in that it is an independent union for workers only. While the only agricultural labourers' strike that I heard about, was the annual ritual strike to mark May Day, the brick workers went on strike twice during my stay in the village: demanding higher wages and to protest the mistreatment of a worker. The brick factory owner had tried to scuttle the strikes by bringing in workers from outside the village, but according to the union activists outsiders too joined the strikes. The brick factory workers' union also raised the issue of equal wages for women and men, but to date the payments have not been equalized, whereas agricultural labourers, despite their more consensual approach, have gained equal wages.

The Left Front's bias towards peasants reflects the fact that it was the middle peasants who introduced Communism to rural West Bengal by mobilizing the lower classes against the predominantly landed village elite, who was allied with Congress (Mallick 1993: 130; see also Bhattacharya 1999 on the Left Front's support of the middle peasants). Bandyopadhyay (2003) notes that the Left Front had few other alternatives; it had to mobilize the middle peasants when it suddenly needed to build its base in the rural areas from scratch. In turn, the middle and upper peasantry seized the opportunity to replace the authority of the older rural aristocracy. Consequently, the rise of the Left Front in West Bengal institutionalized the shift of power from absentee landlords towards the rich and middle peasants. The same trend towards the consolidation of power in favour of rich peasants applies to the rest of rural India. It is the result of the Central Government's policies, of the abolition of the zamindari system in 1955 and of the implementation of the Land Ceiling Act in the 1960s (Rogaly, Harriss-White and Bose 1999: 24). The result was the decline of ex-zamindar *bhadralalok*, the non-cultivating and absentee landowners, and the rise of the *chasi*, the landowning, self-cultivating peasants.

In West Bengal, the effective implementation of the land ceiling began in 1967 when the United Front government came to power. The Left Front continued the removal of loopholes and the implementation of the land ceiling legislation. Mallick (1993) argues that the importance of the Left Front land reforms is diminished by their insignificance in terms of total cultivable land. The National Sample Survey data reveal that 3 per cent of the cropped area of West Bengal was redistributed during the land reform (Gazdar and Sengupta 1997). In a West Bengal village studied by Lieten (1992: 43), Scheduled Caste families (49.7 per cent of the population) owned only 7.5 per cent of the land after the implementation of the land reform. Moreover, the much discussed redistribution of ceiling surplus land under the Left Front government after 1977 was quantitatively less significant than the preceding one carried out by the Congress government (Gazdar and Sengupta 1997).

Operation Barga, the securing of sharecroppers' tenancy rights, has had a limited effect because sharecropping has been on the decline; the agricultural labourers outnumber sharecroppers in West Bengal (Mallick 1993: 49, 50). The proportion of land under share tenancy at the time of the reform was approximately 7 per cent (Gazdar and Sengupta 1999). The recording of sharecropper's rights has been slow during the Left Front rule: 1.3 million sharecroppers were listed during the previous land settlement by the Congress party in 1962-65; by September 1985, after eight years of Left Front rule, the figure stood at 1,329,087 (Mallick 1993: 55).

Before independence, two landowners owned most of the arable village land, but there are no longer absentee landowners of large holdings in Janta. In my sample (N = 44) of landowners interviewed, 43 per cent were marginal landowners, 34 per cent small, 13 per cent middle and 9 per cent large.[1] Adapting Mallick's (1993: 39) definition of farmers in West Bengal, I define the landowners who own less than four bighas as marginal and those who own 4-9 bighas as small. I base the cut-off point between the small and marginal on the basis of the villagers' declaration that four to five bighas of land are required to support a household of four to five persons. Consequently, all marginal as well as small farmers with large households are compelled to supplement their income by wage labour. I classify as middle farmers those who own 10-20 bighas and those owning more than 20 bighas as owners of large holdings. Any landless farmer or those owning less than 3 bighas (1 acre) of land is considered eligible to receive 0.5-3 bighas (0.16-1 acre) of land. However, the plots given are usually only 0.5 bigha and not large enough to support even a small family. The great majority of the landless in Janta are yet to receive their share since the government lacks land for distribution. Of the 108 Scheduled Caste men of Janta, only 13 per cent own land and 5 per cent are sharecroppers (author's own census 2004).

In fact, other panchayat schemes have done more for the landless than what the land reform has done. All who are landless are eligible for the following benefits through the panchayats: loans to start small businesses, assistance for widows and elderly people, as well as people unable to work, a small maternity benefit, and a pension saving scheme.

RECORD GROWTH

Despite the apparent limits of the Left Front reforms, most commentators also note positive trends. Even Mallick (1993: 133), who is highly critical of Left Front policies, admits that the Bengali village leadership has gone further in mobilizing the lower classes against the dominant landed elite than elsewhere in India. Rogaly, Harriss-White and Bose (1999: 13) credit West

Bengal with pioneering the implementation of panchayat raj in 1978: arranging local elections and distributing power and resources to village councils. In contrast to the pessimism of most earlier studies on Left Front rule, the later evaluations of the Left Front performance have had to explain the unexpected positive development of rapid economic growth in rural West Bengal. After decades of stagnation, the agricultural production in West Bengal reached the highest growth rate among all the Indian states: 6.9 per cent in the period 1981-82 to 1991-92 (Gazdar and Sengupta 1999: 61). As Gazdar and Sengupta note, the acceleration of agricultural productivity also occurred in Bihar and Orissa, West Bengal's neighbouring states, but West Bengal's growth was the strongest of the three (ibid: 66). They suggest that Left Front reforms might have indirectly contributed to the record growth in the state.

As Bandyopadhyay (2003) points out, the disappearance of the absentee large landowners after the implementation of land ceiling laws was an important prerequisite for the growth. The new owner-cultivators have increased the quantity of arable land brought into effective farming. It is generally agreed that other factors responsible for the record growth include the adoption of higher yielding crop varieties and private investment in irrigation. The latter has enabled the growing of two to three crops of paddy per year in comparison with the previous single crop (Rogaly, Harriss-White and Bose 1999: 20). The Central Government too has contributed to the rise in the peasants' income through low taxation of agricultural production and by subsidizing pesticide and fertilizers (Mallick 1993: 106). However, as Hill (2003) notes, development has in fact occurred unevenly throughout West Bengal so that areas with low potential for irrigation, such as Purulia, western parts of Bankura and Midnapur, have lagged behind the regions with higher water tables. The villagers of Janta experienced the strongest growth in agricultural production in the 1990s when the agricultural production growth rate for the entire state had already reached a plateau.

My observations do not support the view of the Left Front government as an effective distributor of benefits to landowners. The main sources of credit in Janta are private moneylenders and the co-operative bank established long before the Left Front reforms occurred. Nor can the Left Front be credited with the recent improvements in irrigation. There are a few large-scale irrigation systems in West Bengal; no Janta farmer relies on state-built irrigation facilities. The first farmer in Janta to buy an irrigation pump did so in the 1960s when the machines were still heavy and too expensive for small farmers. The inexpensive movable pump sets were introduced in the village in the mid-1980s and became common in the 1990s. These pump sets, which cost Rs.16,000 for the latest and most compact Honda model and Rs.5,000 for a second hand, older model, are within the reach of small and marginal farmers. The newly available irrigation for distant fields brought about new investments in barren lands that could be purchased cheap and employed in paddy cultivation.

The intensification of agriculture has provided landless labourers with considerably more employment opportunities than during earlier decades. Unlike in Punjab, Haryana, and western Uttar Pradesh, where the average farm size is bigger, the rise in productivity in West Bengal has raised the living standards of the rural majority because the intensification of agriculture has so far not led to large-scale, labour-displacing mechanization. Janta and its surrounding regions have also witnessed the growth of a thriving brick industry, thanks to both the region's alluvial soil and the growing demand for bricks as the newly prosperous farmers are replacing their mud houses with brick houses. A few other new factories offer jobs in the region, too.

Finding vacant land in West Bengal, the most densely populated state of India, where the ruling party's popularity has largely been based on its support to small and marginal farmers, is difficult. The state government has boosted the development of new industries on the basis of the Land Acquisition Act which was passed during the colonial regime and gives the state a right to redeem land for public purposes. The state's decisive role in carrying out the land deals has meant that the farmers get paid less from their land than they would if the price was determined through direct negotiations between the industries and landowners.

Massive protests accompanied land acquisitions in Singur near Kolkata where land was obtained at the market price, whereas land was acquired for a steel factory at below market price from Darika near Janta. Working conditions are dismal in this factory, which the CPI(M) promoted; the plant blatantly violates the labour laws. Those small and marginal farmers who had to give up their land but who were not given jobs in return were not only reduced to poverty but have also been exposed to major health hazards. The factory's dust and acid smog cover the adjacent village and farming lands. As Narain (2008) points out, the increase in the price of steel has led to new steel factories springing up in India without proper environmental checks being carried out.

Opposition parties have given a voice to the rural protests against the land acquisitions but they have not caused the conflicts. The protests originate from the real worries and crises caused by the farmers' loss of their livelihood and healthy environment. As I will elaborate, farming in present day rural West Bengal is far from lucrative for small and marginal farmers. They do realize the value of new jobs–provided that they benefit more than they lose.

FROM GROWTH TO CRISES

Subsistence farming on a small plot carries many risks, which the government's subsidy of kerosene, fertilizer and pesticide had greatly alleviated for the past two decades. Since the irrigation pump sets run on kerosene, the profitability of paddy cultivation is now heavily dependent on its price. The price increased slowly in the 1990s, but in 2000 the world price of oil shot up just when the Indian government partly reduced its kerosene subsidy. The price of kerosene rose from Rs.10 to Rs.18, which was a shock to

Janta's small farmers, many of whom decided not to sow the spring crop.

Since the launch of the economic reforms by the Central Government in the early 1990s, there was growing pressure on the state to make substantial changes to its agricultural policies. India's acceptance of the treaties which emerged from the Uruguay Round negotiations has led, since the 1990s, to pressure for liberalization and globalization of agriculture. However, since India has subsidized its agriculture much less than most Western nations, there has been no great pressure to reduce the subsidies significantly. Nevertheless, state investment in agriculture and rural areas fell, and the prices of agricultural produce have no longer kept up with the rising costs of farming. It was no wonder that the BJP's defeat in the 2004 general elections was generally attributed to the rural population's discontent. The Congress-led government has sought to maintain its rural electorate by launching the Rural Employment Guarantee programme and a loan waiver for small farmers. Neither programme addresses the underlying cause of the agricultural crises in India: farmers' decreasing profits due to the rising cost of farming and low market prices.

Economic growth, when mainly derived from the expansion of irrigation, has its limits. Once most areas suitable for cultivation are covered, growth will slow down. As pointed out by the 'Commentary', *Economic and Political Weekly* (2003), in some years (1998-99 and 1999-2000) the growth was negative and in two years (1995-96 and 1999-2000) it was no more than 1.4 and 1.6 per cent. The decline in production is attributed to the fragmentation of land, which hinders technological development.

The small and marginal farmers in Janta identify their decline in agricultural production as deriving from the change in the price ratio between their produce and the cost of farming. The price ratios were most profitable around 1996-97, but since then the price of rice has decreased, while the growing supply of vegetables has decreased their market price. The food department subsidizes rice farmers by buying at higher than market prices, but because the department buys rice through rice-millers, this money does not fully reach the producers.

By 2003, rice farming plunged into a full-blown crisis. When the price of paddy went down from Rs.640 per quintal in 1999 to Rs.340 at its lowest, irrigated crops were producing losses instead of profits. Ghosh and Harriss-White (2002) describe the crisis as evolving from the state-level differences in the political control of agricultural cost structures both within India and Asia. As a result of the reforms of the central state, it is now possible to import and export grain between the various Indian states, which nevertheless to a certain degree retain the authority to decide on subsidies to their farmers. Due to state level differences in subsidies, cheap rice now finds it way to West Bengal from Bihar. At the same time, the global liberalization of the rice market has diminished the West Bengal farmers' previous markets in Bangladesh, Nepal and Bhutan, because these regions are now able to import cheaper rice from other Asian countries.

In the winter of 2004, the Janta farmers sold a quintal of paddy for Rs.460. The large village landowners could cope with this price level and produce paddy for the market through the larger volume of their production, whereas marginal and small farmers shifted to cultivating rice for their own consumption. Since irrigation has also made intensified vegetable farming possible, small and marginal farmers shifted to earning cash from growing vegetables, especially potatoes. Even landowners are now increasingly seeking jobs outside agriculture or starting small-scale businesses which have become more viable, thanks to the building of the mobile phone networks (see Chapter 1).

In 2005 the price of paddy rose so that irrigated crops once again became slightly profitable. But because of the upward trend in the price of kerosene, a substantial rise in farmers' incomes depends on the pace of the electrification of rural West Bengal. Since all irrigation pumps can be run either on kerosene or electricity, those farmers whose fields are located in areas where the state has provided access to electricity have shifted to running their irrigation pumps on electricity. However, at present, by far most of the fields do not have access to electricity.

Despite the setbacks in the economic growth, many small and middle landowners, especially families with more sons than daughters, have been able to increase the amount of their landholdings since land is often purchased with dowry payments or even given as part of a dowry. In 1999 I was told that the groom's parents could demand a dowry of Rs.20,000 per bigha of their land. Middle and large peasants (owning more than 10 bighas) can build large cemented houses, purchase electricity and televisions and buy motorcycles and even cars. It is these newly prosperous middle peasants and the upper caste new entrepreneurs (shopkeepers, poultry farmers, and owners of transport businesses) who have challenged the power of the elite families (the leading village communists), providing the backing for the rise of the new opposition party, the BJP, in the village. The opposition is therefore gaining ground by using the same methods with which the Left Front once gained power: using the newly prosperous peasants to challenge the old elite. Both power struggles, the rise of the Left Front and the new opposition to the Left Front, follow the conclusion reached by Nicholas (1966: 56) that the dispersal of resources can increase the number of competing centres of power.

One would suppose, as Basu (2001) does, that the disillusioned landless would form the backbone of the new opposition to the Left Front. However, despite the limits of land reform, the landless low castes were not among the first to join the opposition to the Left Front in Janta. On the contrary, at present they form the backbone of the support for the Left Front in the village and speak about a remarkable improvement in their caste's position, while the middle farmers, who gained most under Left Front rule, are challenging the party. In the light of the critical evaluation of the Left Front reforms, which have shown the disadvantaged position of the low castes in relation to the landowners, these reactions exemplify the difficulties of explaining political behaviour on the basis of statistically measured factors. The villagers' political views are related to their position in the social structure, but not in a mechanically predictable way: understanding political action requires attention to the way politics and political goals are perceived. I will next explore how Janta's different castes and classes perceive the recent decade's development. The villagers' understanding of politics will be the topic of Chapter 3.

I gained insights into the village's recent history through interviews and informal discussions. I started by questioning the villagers on the kind of changes *(bodol)* they had witnessed in the village, but soon noticed that they responded better when I rephrased the question to ask what kind of development *(unnoti, poriborton)* they had experienced in the village and within their caste. As Gupta (1998: 33) argues, the discourses of development are an inescapable feature of the everyday life in contemporary northern India. According to Gupta, the postcolonial period in India is characterized by a distinctive relationship between modernity and development, which serves as the chief legitimizing function of ruling regimes and the state. The 'modern' as a celebration of Western progress, civilization, rationality, and development was instituted as a global phenomenon by colonialism. After the demise of colonialism, the chief premises of modernity, such as the belief in teleological narratives, were continued through development discourses. Gupta carries on, exploring how different interest groups in India have argued for different development measures, demonstrating how a discourse he labelled Orientalistic can be contentiously redeployed. Indeed, the great variation and changes in even the general definitions of development show that Orientalism is just one strand of the development discourse. I will next turn to explore the local understandings of development, instead of its many general definitions, in order to understand the villagers' political motivations which are, to a large extent, locally authored.

SEIZING DEVELOPMENT: *KHAUA, MAKHA, PORA*

By no means does the recent agricultural growth in West Bengal present a new phenomenon. A long agrarian cycle of growth in

Mughal and nawabi Bengal came to a catastrophic end with the great famine of 1770. Agricultural production recovered in the subsequent decades. Even the rule of the East India Company from 1770-1860 presented a period of growth in almost all parts of Bengal despite its negative impacts on the local economy and society. From 1881-1981 the old Bengal Presidency, and later West Bengal, suffered stagnation (Bandyopadhyay 2003: 1).

In Janta, many consumer items became common only after India gained independence. A wife of a self-taught doctor, who moved to Janta in 1944, says their house was the first in the village to offer tea. The doctor's bicycle was the first vehicle in the village. Since then bicycles, tea and soap have become common items, roads have been improved, regular bus services now connect the villages, and state investments are evident in the improved accessibility of schools and public health services.

However, the past decade marks a decisive phase in the villagers' experience of growth and economic prosperity. When I asked villagers what kind of unnoti they had experienced, both the small landowners and landless said that they no longer had to endure regular periods of starvation and food scarcity that were common only a decade ago. Earlier, I was told, the blooming of the Simul tree would mark the beginning of a period of food scarcity. 'One can now feed one's family if one is working,' said a low caste Bagdi woman. The following excerpts from interviews illustrate the villagers' experiences of the new affluence:

> *Do you mean that the village is now far more developed than before?*
> It is much better than than earlier. Then when I did not have money to buy food, I could make only a rupee by working for the rich farmers. It was not possible to fill one's stomach with just a rupee's worth of food. It was difficult to raise children on such a meagre income. I could not educate them. Our parents could not send us to school.
>
> Nowadays the government helps by distributing schoolbooks. It helps in many ways. There is no more poverty *(abhab)*. Nowadays, there is no poverty if one works. If I make a thousand bricks at the

factory, I earn Rs.100. If both of us work, there is no poverty and we can even save some money. The government offers assistance (*sahajyo*) to those who cannot work. For instance, the government gives seeds to those who have a little land but cannot afford to sow. —A Bagdi man

What kind of unnoti *have you seen in the village in your lifetime?*
Earlier I saw very little development, but now there is a lot.

What kind of development?
Earlier there was no *boro* crop. There was only one crop of paddy a year. I could not feed my children. Now that I grow two crops, I can feed my children and sell rice for Rs.20, 000. —A woman from a Tili landowning family

What kind of development has taken place in agriculture?
There has been a lot of development. Those who own a pump set for irrigation have experienced the most development. But we who have to pay Rs.30 per hour (to rent the pump set for irrigation) have not seen any development. We remain the same.

Before there was only one crop, now there are two crops. The result is that work is available. Everyone has become equal *(shobai ek hoye gechhe)*. Nowadays one can speak to everyone. Earlier this was not possible. The wage earner and the *bhadrolok* [the respectable people, the upper class] have become the same. I can talk to you and another person can talk to me. It was not like this before. There was fear.

What kind of development have you seen in the village?
The environment has improved. Earlier farmers did not have that much money and now farmers are working harder and growing two crops of paddy. Now farmers have more money and the village has developed *(poriborton bhalo hoechhe)*. Now farmers have an income at all times. They grow paddy and various kinds of vegetables.

> *What kind of development is necessary for women?*
> I hope that women will live happily. They should have food, clothes to wear and oil to use on their skin. They should be able to raise their sons and be happy. –A woman from a Tili landowning family

> Everything is good now. During festivals, we can go out looking like the bhadrolok (respectable people, middle class). In hard times we had to wear thick clothes and eat coarse rice (*mota kapor, mota bhat*). I went through such hardship that I wore saris worth Rs.15. Now even men dress well. Earlier, we did not have soap to wash dirty clothes with, but now we do. These days we cannot get by without using soap, and when we dress well, nobody recognizes us as Bagdis. We go out together with other women, like ladies. –A Bagdi woman

Development is experienced and talked about as the improved ability to earn enough to feed one's family. At the same time the new affluence is conceptualized as part of the broader cultural standard of living, often captured by the expressions khaua, makha, pora, (eating, rubbing of oil, clothing), which sum up the bare essentials of life. One can eat twice a day (as opposed to having rice only once a day) with a greater variety of vegetables and better quality rice (as opposed to coarse rice, *mota bhat*) than before. Women no longer have to wear the epitome of poverty–thick *(mota)* saris. Women recalled that these cheap and durable saris, which can still be found in the market, were uncomfortably hot and so heavy that it was difficult to get out of the river after bathing (women bathe with their saris on). Now even the poorer women have shifted to wearing finer saris, and they can afford to have a fresh sari in reserve for special occasions, such as visits outside the village. They can also afford soap for washing and oil to rub on their skin after bathing.

Some of the interviewees included good relationships and a good environment in their description of development. For the middle and large landowners, this includes access to electricity, fans, televisions, motorcycles and living in brick or concrete houses in addition to proper food, dress and soap.

All segments of the village society have prospered, but the pace has not been equal for all. Even as the small farmers and landless peasants have prospered, they have lagged behind the middle and large farmers. Many Bagdis reply to the question on recent change with 'it is the same, we just work the whole time', or 'we work and yet have no property'. Bagdis not only compare their position with the new prosperity of the landowning villagers, especially the Tilis, but also find that some Bagdis have benefited more than others. After all, only a minority of the landless peasants has received land, and only the poorest have received considerable assistance from the panchayat. A few poor Bagdi families have been provided with houses (through government funding, the scheme is called 'Indira houses'), to the envy of some villagers who complain about getting nothing from the government but vaccinations.

The scarcity of khaua, makha, pora is experienced physically and socially. A Tili woman who experienced periods of food scarcity told me that during those times she used to avoid calling on others, fearing that people might think she was on the look out for a free meal. Another Tili woman compared her present position to her past state of poverty: 'Now that my sons are working and earning, when I go to anyone's house, they say, Kakima (aunt) have some *muri* (puffed rice) or rice. Earlier, when I went to visit they would say she has come for food.' It is possible to deduce from a person's appearance–his or her dress and general health–whether he/she lacks the proper khaua, makha, pora. The new ability to maintain a standard of living translates into pride, not only in oneself, but also in one's caste status.

CASTE, CLASS, AND AFFLUENCE

Despite the relative discontent of the landless and small landowners, there is a widespread agreement that the gap between the different village strata, between the high and low castes, has narrowed. The brahmins note that the Tili caste's pride has increased and Tilis point out the same change within the lower castes. Left Front policies and new job opportunities have lessened the landless labourers' dependency on landowners, and Bagdis comment on the remarkable improvement in their caste position:

> We are Bagdis, but now we can go to the house of *didi* [an older woman, literally, older sister, from a caste superior to hers]. There has been a lot of change. I can give a brahmin a glass of water. Previously they did not take water from our hands. When I am able to give a didi a cup of tea that shows the development of people. –A Bagdi woman

> Nowadays it does not matter if there is touching, since it is possible to wash the pollution off. It is possible to go and eat in higher caste houses without having to wash the metal utensils oneself. Earlier, one had to eat in a separate place and wash the plate one ate off. People's way of thinking has changed. Before, rich people did not care if poor people could not afford to eat or wear proper clothes. Now everybody has become the same. You eat and I eat too. Yes, they have realized that they need our labour and must not keep a distance. Now they have no way but to treat us better. –A Bagdi man

Yet, caste remains one of a villager's primary identities. News from other villages is always told in relation to the caste identity of the people involved. Villagers know one another's caste identity, while a stranger's caste identity is inferred on the basis of his dialect, behaviour, or deduced from one's clothing.

Issues of pollution and touching are the key principles by which villagers perceive caste: 'Here we have caste discrimination *(amader eikhane jater bichar kare)*, Didi. We do not touch the Bauris, or Muslims. No Tili touches us,' a Bagdi woman explained about caste. Caste discrimination *(jater bichar)* entails the prevention of pollution through contact with the lower castes.

Caste purity is chiefly maintained by caste endogamy and avoiding touching or sitting on the same level as a lower caste person, receiving cooked food from a lower caste, or touching the dishes which a lower caste person had used. Villagers justified caste discrimination on the grounds that others would disapprove of them if they did not follow the rules. Moreover, polluting a higher caste person is considered a sin.

Higher castes seldom visit the lower caste neighbourhoods. Lower castes enter higher caste neighbourhoods as day labourers, to sell fish and vegetable or just chat. The category friends (*bondhu*) is reserved for one's lower caste acquaintances whereas kinship terms are used to address one's neighbours or the people of one's own neighbourhood (who belong to same caste). Lower caste friends are invited to family weddings but they come to the marriage dinner only after one's *bhaiat* (kin group delineated by seven generations of ancestors on the father's side), *bari* (kin group originally sharing a house) and *para atmio* (kin group sharing the same neighbourhood). When lower castes visit higher caste homes, they usually stand or sit in the yard, without entering the house. Lower caste labourers have their meals on the veranda as part of their payment, but never enter the higher caste house. Higher castes do not have food at lower caste houses. They may have tea, but even this is considered an unusually liberal gesture. Bagdis usually declined to offer me tea, only to regret not having offered anything after I had shown my reformist attitude by raising questions about Bagdi experiences and views of caste. Usually my assistant Asima rejected the idea of having tea in lower caste households and was visibly nervous after we did drink tea; Asima's husband was present at the time and encouraged us to do so.

When brahmins invite Tilis to a meal at their house on a special occasion, Tilis have to pay for the food to indicate their lower position in the caste hierarchy. Bagdi workers can eat in higher caste households, but they usually have to wash the plate they had eaten off in order to avoid polluting their hosts. My assistant always took care to wash the cups the two of us drank from when we had tea in brahmin households, so my level of impurity was determined by my contact with the Tilis.

Ideas of purity and pollution prevail in the village but do so in a very different setting compared to the times when low castes were dependent on a few prosperous landowners of the dominant caste. Service relationships between castes have become secondary to market relationships, and no single large landowner can act as the highest authority in the village.

With the exception of the Tilis, members of different castes do not meet to discuss disputes as a community. Even now the Tili committee (*samiti*) tries to sort out disputes, but its verdicts are considered less binding than those of the party. The head of the Tili committee himself stressed that the caste committee is separate from politics. The main tasks of the caste association are to give advice when families divide their property and organize religious festivals (*pujas*). When I asked the villagers whether the Tili samiti ever discusses breaches of caste purity, I was told that the maintenance of caste purity is up to the individual households. Instead of a particular community supervising caste discrimination, caste practices are debated in various arenas. Moreover, the opportunities for inter-caste socializing which start in the primary schools, where children of all castes have their midday meal (sponsored by the Central Government) together, have increased.

My Tili hosts were not too strongly opposed to my wish to visit lower caste neighbourhoods, except that initially they were worried about my safety. Tilis cannot eat in a Bagdi house but I sensed they were pleased to hear that I had eaten a meal in a Bagdi house where I attended a wedding ceremony. And what created the greatest approval for me—among all castes—was helping to arrange a free heart operation (valve replacement) for a Bagdi man at Dr. Devi Shetty's charitable clinic.

The relationships between higher and lower castes are not merely about the higher group's desire to keep a distance from the polluting lower castes. There are also signs of increased tolerance even towards transgressions of caste rules. Despite the nearly complete adherence to caste endogamy, the possibility of inter-caste marriages enters discussions. It is common knowledge in the village that inter-caste marriages do take place in urban areas and a few villagers have relatives living in urban areas who have entered inter-caste marriages. One Bagdi man, a CPI(M) activist, even wished for an end to caste endogamy:

> *What do you think should be done about caste discrimination?*
> It should be stopped so that we can unite. We must unite. It would be convenient for us. No one should practise untouchability or consider another person as unimportant. If somebody outside the community were to marry a Tili girl, it would cause havoc. It is not easy to understand this, both rich and poor do it . . . Affairs happen between high and low castes, at school or while working in other people's houses, for instance. People do not accept it. Everybody marries within his or her own caste. I hope a time will come when this will change.

There were signs that caste discrimination was on the wane, but the change did not seem as overwhelming as the Bagdis described. Their exaggeration of the changes expresses their aspirations, awareness of the new opportunities as well as their new sense of pride. There are no wealthy Bagdis in Janta, but the villagers know of low caste people outside Janta who have became so influential that 'even brahmins have food in their house'. They know that the low caste status does not prevent one from rising to the upper class. Their emphasis on being able to sit on the same level with others and not having to wash their utensils in higher caste houses for fear of polluting the host shows that they see these aspects of caste discrimination as most humiliating.

Many villagers are aware that caste discrimination is wrong and also know the arguments for ending it, but tend to be more liberal in their speech than in behaviour. Tili women criticized Bagdis for their impure habits, but they also went as far as to admit that they followed caste rules for the sake of living in society. They say that in their heart they know it is wrong. Most of these women had been to school and read about the anti-caste ideas of Hindu reformists such as Swami Vivekananda. At school they had met children from different caste groups and even made friends with them. One woman admitted having taken *prasad* (food offerings to the Gods and Goddesses) from a Bagdi at a temple 'because prasad is from God', while another Tili woman was horrified at the idea of consuming a *pitha* (a pancake-like preparation made as a part of the annual harvest rituals) offered by a Bagdi. A Tili man who was invited to have a meal at a brahmin house and paid for the food to demonstrate his inferiority, expressed his anger at the practice, but did so only after he was back in his own house.

When an elderly brahmin man came to see me unexpectedly at Asima's house, the women of the household fled to sit in another corner of the veranda and did not offer him tea. I felt awkward at having been left alone with him, and Asima's husband later scolded the women for not offering the man tea. As an educated person with a government job in Vishnupur, he was eager to present his rational outlook on life to me, including the fact that he was against caste discrimination. Looking pleased—a lower caste woman bowed down in front of him, touching his feet to signify her subservience to him—he told me that caste practices continue because simple village people like to maintain their age-old habits. But he also admitted that although his work with the health department took him to different caste neighbourhoods, he never ate cooked food in the houses that he visited. In his own house he looked unhappy when a Tili woman sat on the same level as him and he made his intentions clear by gesturing her to move from the bench that we were sharing. He explained the necessity of keeping a distance from the lower castes by using a 'scientific' argument: people from the lower castes did not maintain as strict a hygienic standard as he did.

The high and low castes in Janta do share an understanding and knowledge of what impurity entails. But as Mencher (1975) pointed out, those who are placed higher in the hierarchy go to great lengths to justify and rationalize the system, presenting explicit or implicit self-doubt about the premise of caste. Had a complete consensus prevailed in Janta, the justifications would have been unnecessary. I found ideas of purity and pollution existing simultaneously with those of the deplorable nature of caste discrimination and how it was on the wane. It is possible that the debates and the ambivalence regarding caste are creating space for change in dominant caste practices, such as caste endogamy in marriage (as has happened in urban India).

I heard of two cases of inter-caste marriage in Janta. A Chasa man had married a lower caste, Napit, a widow. The marriage was criticized because it was an inter-caste one, and also because the woman had had to abandon her children from her first marriage after marrying the Chasa man for love. Nevertheless, the couple was able to live in Janta, although not in the main Chasa neighbourhood. Instead they lived in a neighbourhood where members of both Tati and Napit castes lived. A more recent inter-caste marriage took place between a Chasa girl and a Tili boy. Chasas are regarded as lower than Tilis, but perhaps because the distance is not too great, the union had merely caused astonishment and no major opposition in the village. There still were no marriages between the Scheduled and upper castes and many were of the opinion that these unions would not be tolerated in the village. A Tili family had a relative in another village who had married a Bagdi girl. This relative's family had reacted to the marriage by selling their property and leaving the village.

Sanskritization, which views lower castes as rising in status by adopting upper caste practices, has explained the pattern of change in caste relations, particularly within the middle castes. In Janta, striving for a purer lifestyle did not appear to be a prime motivation. One change that parallels sanskritization is that of Bagdi women giving up drinking locally made wine on the night of the Poush festival (festival of the winter harvest). Many Tilis told me how Bagdi women would gather to sing and drink in strategic sites so that others, even higher caste women, could easily gather to watch the event. On the night of the Poush festival we had to search hard to find a small group of Bagdis who still practised the tradition of singing and wine drinking–most Bagdi women had stayed at home. 'Bagdi women are becoming respectable (*bhadra*),' I was told.

Wine drinking presents a departure from a pure life style; however, women are also said to be striving for bhadra, upper class identity. Lower castes talked about imitating the upper strata of the village society in terms of consumption: being able to eat and dress so well that they cannot be recognized as low. On the one hand, they circumvent the purity criteria for social ascent by striving for a new identity through higher levels of consumption. On the other hand, villagers perceive the new affluence as contributing to the collective sense of pride in one's caste.

Caste is a social reality in the village, but it is not perceived as unchanging or one's sole form of identity. The villagers also recognize class positions, although class differences follow caste lines, and in daily interaction people observe the caste differences. Most Tilis own land, most of the few village brahmins have white-collar jobs and most low caste people are daily labourers. Even the low castes and landless farmers who received land from the government still depend on wage labour to supplement their income from their small plots. Caste is the more prominent form of identity in the village when compared with urban areas. In the Kolkata working class neighbourhood where I did fieldwork in the 1990s (Tenhunen 2003), people seldom identified others predominantly in terms of caste; inter-caste arranged marriages were common, and neighbourhoods were not caste-based.

In Janta class is recognized most by the Tilis among whom there is most class differentiation: those who own enough land and need not work as a labourers are considered superior to those compelled to work as daily labourers. Everybody recognizes people who have white-collar jobs as upper class, bhadralok. Even low caste, salaried people are considered as belonging to the upper class, bhadralok, whom, I was told, even the brahmins accept. Tili women mentioned that my acceptance in the village by higher caste people—they allowed me to sit on the same level as they—was influenced by class, my status as an educated, wealthy (they presumed that as a westerner, I had to be wealthy) person.

The villagers' emphasis on consumption, khaua, makha, pora, instead of striving for a pure lifestyle, indicates that one's identity indeed draws from more than one's ritual status based on ideas of purity. Better standards of khaua, makha, pora are conceptualized according to the cultural criteria for class identity and especially the bhadralok lifestyle. Reaching new consumption levels is the lower castes' way of social climbing, which helps circumvent purity issues: they do not imitate the high castes' pure habits and thereby confirm the high value of purity, nor do they directly threaten the caste hierarchy. Attaining new levels of consumption emphasizes one's class identity, besides contributing to the collective pride in one's caste.

As Schneider (1980) pointed out, gender, class, and kinship connect through the concepts of personhood. The discourses I have looked at in this chapter—body, caste and class—are interlinked because they all ultimately refer to concepts of personhood. Consequently, rather than doing away with other identities, improvements in any one of these attributes can contribute to the others by leading to a reinterpretation of all the interconnected attributes that build up one's status. Although acquiring a higher status by earning more does not influence one's purity and the ritual status, it can influence the collective pride in one's caste group. In turn, the new pride can motivate caste members to question the cultural code of conduct based on the ideas of purity.

Changing caste equations in Janta entails contradictory and heterogeneous trends. Instead of a communal organ supervising caste purity, the tenets of caste discrimination are debated in various settings, producing heterogeneous interpretations which show in the increasing tolerance of transgressions and critical discourses. Like any other cultural identity, caste entails a shared understanding of one another's differences, but the shared understanding of caste does not prevent the villagers from perceiving how callous caste logic is towards the lower castes. There is space for negotiating the extreme to which one has to go to avoid impurity as well as for criticizing the tenets of caste. Although Janta's spatial and social structure show few signs of change–the castes live in separate neighbourhoods, being low caste also means being working class and lagging behind the upper castes' consumption levels–the gap between different classes in the village has narrowed. Labourers, small and middle farmers, have been able to attain higher living standards (khaua, makha pora). Development is perceived, practised and put on display as a bodily process, concerning the essences of personhood (khaua, makha, pora) and linked with other discourses on personhood. Development is, at the same time, experienced as a new emphasis on class identity as well as increased collective pride in one's caste.

One central feature of the new class and caste relationships is that instead of depending on a few large landowners, the labourers now negotiate with the landowners through institutions led by the Left Front. The caste-based authority has eroded, thanks to the new economic and political avenues, but the shift has not meant moving away from a caste-based order towards the rule of the workers, nor towards an individualistic ideology of the representative democracy.

NOTE

1 The proportion of marginal landowners in Janta is close to that of the village of Torkotala, 49 per cent (N = 47), in the neighbouring district of Bankura, in Midnapur district studied by Davis (1983: 101). The proportion is, however, lower than the figures presented by Williams (1999: 241) of three villages in Birbhum district: 69 per cent (N = 91) and 84 per cent (N = 38 and 100) for two villages. In the village in Birbhum district studied by Lieten (1992: 53), only 12 per cent (N = 73) of the landowners were marginal.

THREE

Village Politics

As Östör (1984) argues, the modernization of the system of local government and the introduction of the market system have induced changes in rural Bengal, but have not led to a separation of politics, religion and the economy according to Western notions of governance. Nevertheless, I start my examination of the local political domain by taking a look at the system of local governance, since it is a crucial part of the political sphere. I shall interpret the local understanding of the political, exploring how it enables critical discourses and how it is linked to national parties and state-led institutions and reforms. I shall also consider how the local political domain relates to gender (see also Chapter 4).

A wealthy Tili family, the Kundus, enjoyed great authority in Janta for most of the twentieth century. They once owned 56 acres of land, which the father of the present male head of the family had received in return for services rendered and favours done for a zamindar. Mr. Kundu, his father, elder brother and daughter have all represented the village in the local governing bodies. Mr. Kundu says of his father, 'If my father said a word, the whole village responded. They knew him as the big man (*boro babu*). If somebody dared to stand up against him, the whole village would beat up that person. That is why the village is now so well developed. Everybody listened to him.' One can sense that he is lamenting the loss of the family's position of power even more than the loss of its wealth. He now owns four acres of land. The previous local election was the first since India's independence in which no family member was a candidate. Janta no longer has a single village leader.

Janta now belongs to the joint panchayat (village council) of sixteen adjacent villages. The main role of the panchayat is to handle the allocation of resources for development purposes, which includes the distribution of land to the landless. In practice, land distribution has been halted because of a lack of vested land, which the government would have acquired from farmers whose landownership exceeds the land ceiling. Through the panchayat, Janta has received money for building of tube wells, a school, an atchala, as well as road improvements. Each village is allocated money for public works and the way this money would be put to use is decided at annual village meetings where all the villagers (men and women across castes) gather. The panchayat also provides assistance for widows and elderly people, runs a pension saving scheme for day labourers, gives loans and helps poor farmers by distributing seeds and money to invest in farming. Individual requests for panchayat benefits have to be made through the two village representatives. After the introduction of quotas for the low castes and women, Janta's panchayat representatives in the following two elections were a Tili woman and a Baul man. In the panchayat elected in 2003, Janta was represented by two low caste women, since 2007 elections by a woman and a man who are Tilis. During my stay in the village, the panchayat representatives maintained a low profile, while the most powerful people mediating in village disputes were the local party leaders from wealthy families.

STATE AND LOCAL GOVERNANCE

The changes in local government were initiated by state-run policies. Although the outcome of the many reforms is not completely dictated by the state, understanding the local political domain and its dynamism requires looking into the colonial policies as well as the many reforms initiated by the Indian state. Panchayats are the main units of the state-run system of local governance, and were first introduced in independent India in 1959. The British rulers had tried developing local governments to improve administrative efficiency and increase the colonial regime's finances since the 1860s. Provincial autonomy was established under the Government of India Act of 1935. Thereafter, there was an effort to decentralize the administration in independent India by setting up various committees on whose recommendations the individual states passed differing legislations. In 1978, the Ashok Mehta Committee was the first to propose the involvement of political parties in panchayat elections (Rai et al. 2001: 3-12).

West Bengal became the first state in India to implement the election of panchayat members from among competing political parties through universal adult franchise when the Left Front applied the West Bengal Panchayat Act (1973) in 1978 (Lieten 1992: 99-100). The Left Front government introduced three levels of panchayats–block level, district level and village level–responsible for implementing rural development schemes. Panchayats retain the taxes they collect as well as a portion of land revenue, and have control over vested land and water tanks. The block, subdivision and district level bureaucrats are at the panchayat's service. To ensure that panchayats are involved not only in the implementation of policies but also in the formulation thereof, they collaborate with district and block level planning committees (Basu 2002: 333-334). In 1978, the Left Front government decreed that at least two women must serve on each village panchayat. If no women had been elected, they could be nominated. However, women continued to be underrepresented in village panchayats (Basu 1992: 68).

The most recent local government reform was the reservation of panchayat seats for women, Scheduled Castes and Scheduled Tribes, effective in West Bengal since 1993. The reservation of seats was part of prime minister Narasimha Rao's Central Government's effort to establish grassroot-level democracy in rural India. Thanks to the Constitutional (73rd Amendment) Act, which was passed in 1992 and came into force in 1993, three million female representatives were elected to panchayats in rural India, making the reform the world's largest experiment in decentralization of governance (Rai et al. 2001: 11, 18, 29).

The state-established panchayat system is based on the ancient panchayats. Contrary to the common belief that the leading Aryan householders in each village formed the ideal ancient panchayats, it was the village elders invited by the village headman whose hereditary power was based on his landholdings (Wolpert 1989: 360-61). Mughal rule introduced zamindars as an intermediary in a governing position between the ruler and the people, removing some of the village self-government's authority (Rai et al. 2002: 3, citing Khanna 1999). As Mendelsohn (2002: 200) notes, there is a scarcity of research material and observations of local and regional authority across time and region—even during the post-independent period, not to mention the pre-British period—but the available writings on Mughal rule indicate that the Mughal regime dealt indirectly with the village, leaving most judicial matters to village governing organs.

Pre-British India was ruled by local rajas and various intermediaries between the raja and the peasant tillers of the soil whom the emperor had rewarded with zamindari holdings for life. The British East India Company's Permanent Settlement policy changed the economic and social structure of Bengal by making the land the private property of the zamindars, and ignoring the previous relationships between tiller, intermediaries of various kinds and the state (Cohn and Berreman 1971: 80). The measures taken by the Company Raj ruined the Malla kings of Bengal and created a disarray among the hierarchically inferior, among rajas and their immediate land grantees, as well as among the actual cultivators (Östör 1984:167). Although the Permanent Settlement terms did not grant landlords the responsibility for local government, in practice, the British-Indian government left the maintenance of village law and order to the landlords who had the power to hire the village watchmen (Mukhopadhay 1994: 26). The expansion of the court system, since the late nineteenth century, challenged the local authority but did not replace it. The abolition of the zamindari system after Independence presented a major challenge to the landlords' local authority. Village ethnographies, however, offer evidence of a village headmen's substantial power, both in pre-independent and in newly independent India. Nicholas (1998), for example, describes how, in the early 1960s, the head of a village in West Bengal was able to dictate a panchayat election, appoint all the panchayat members and elect himself to the highest position.

POLITICAL TURMOIL IN JANTA AND WEST BENGAL

In Janta there is no longer any sovereign single village leader. The major faction in Janta is headed by one of the largest landowners in the village, who is also a CPI(M) leader. Many of the village disputes were about attempts to compete with and protest against his domination. One such dispute involved a group of newly affluent middle farmers (Tilis) demolishing his video hall one evening. One of the main motivations for the protest was that he had not co-operated with other influential men in arranging a cultural programme in the village. Another reason for the attack was that he had given the Bagdis a permit to keep their cattle on a plot owned by another Tili family, which led to BJP supporters destroying a Bagdi home that same night.

Political parties and their leaders are so powerful in the village that it is said to be impossible to live there without the patronage of one of the rival parties. The power and influence of political parties and their leaders depend on their ability to solve village disputes which, in turn, draws from an understanding of the realm of village politics and power. Meetings (for which the English word is used in the village) of various kinds are considered part of normal village life. Both women and men gather to attend village panchayat meetings, but meetings of the Tili caste association are only for men, who are, in turn, excluded from the women's committee meetings. The fourth type of village meeting involves conflict settlement. Anyone with a grievance could call a village meeting during which a solution would be negotiated among the disputing parties. These meetings could be planned ahead or arranged quite spontaneously. Once I witnessed a fight after which both parties, one after the other, simply went to the atchala to ask for a judgment. Women do not actively participate in these meetings; they are merely allowed to stand apart and listen.

In practice, there were more rumours and talk about possible meetings than actual meetings taking place. Only two village meetings took place during the period I lived in the village. After the stabbing mentioned in the Introduction the men gathered for a meeting called by the BJP party, which successfully availed itself of the murder suspect's position in the Left Front and turned the villagers against his party. Later the victim (who survived a few months before succumbing to his injuries) too planned to call a meeting to reveal the truth about the stabbing. The murder suspect, in turn, planned to call a meeting after an angry mob destroyed his property. The second meeting took place after a riot between the two rival parties: each party had kidnapped two of the rival party's supporters and the meeting was called to decide who would release their prisoners first.

Instead of disputes getting sorted out at a meeting, what can occur is that these end in a fight between rival party supporters or destruction of one another's property. In case party leaders are not able to negotiate a mutually agreeable solution, the dispute can be taken to court. However, the villagers do not have much trust in legal procedures; the police are suspected of being corrupt and inefficient, and many incidents exemplify police inefficiency.

In Janta, Tili men formed a security unit that patrolled the village at night to protect the villagers from theft. Instances of robbery continued, nonetheless: irrigation pump sets were stolen from the fields and one night a clothes shop was robbed of its stock. Once policemen came to the village, wanting to take men suspected of destroying a rival party's property to the police station for interrogation. The villagers said that they would turn in the two men on condition that two policemen remained in the village's custody. The police were not willing to have their men taken hostage by the village, but were not able to assert their authority either, and therefore went back empty-handed.

In May 2000, the police were reported to have stood by, ineffectually, when 5,000 Trinamul party activists attacked a CPI(M)-dominated village in Keshpur, in the Midnapur district. The police did not have adequate forces with which either to stop the attackers or protect the villagers, both men and women, who defended themselves (*Telegraph,* 21 May 2000). An investigation into the rising number of lynchings in the state has revealed that most of them occurred after police had repeatedly failed to arrest a known criminal, or prevent regular criminal activities (Mukherjee 2000).

In March 2007, the West Bengal government witnessed the police's inability to control rural protest in Midnapur district. It had sent police forces to subdue resistance by farmers, against the setting up of a chemical hub in the village of Nandigram. The police could not seize the area from the villagers despite firing at them and killing fourteen villagers. Later in the same year, chief minister Buddhadeb Bhattacharjee sent the party cadres to capture the village, using brute force. This time the news about the rural conflict spread fast through the 24-hour television channels which most of the state population had ample time to watch as they could not go out of their houses because of the ensuing unrest and the general strike announced by the opposition. Almost overnight the chief minister's image was transformed from that of a heroic reformer into a villain whose effigies were burnt on the streets.

Villagers take liberties at times, thanks to the weakness of the police, but they also complain about a lack of protection from the police. Public action in one of the nearby villages illustrates the irony of the situation: the villagers protested against police ineptitude by destroying the police station.

Political turmoil in the village was not considered normal. The Tili women from my neighbourhood repeatedly told me that earlier everyone was united 'as one'. The 'oneness' refers to the Left Front's extended rule since 1977, not only in Janta, but also throughout the state of West Bengal. When the Left Front consolidated its power in West Bengal, the landowners shifted from opposing the movement to supporting it.

The whole village of Janta, including major landowners, middle peasants, and landless labourers used to support the Left Front. They were loyal to the Revolutionary Socialist Party (RSP) and CPI(M) which, together with a few other leftist parties, form the Left Front. This situation resulted from the landowners' gradual realization that joining the movement could be more advantageous than resisting it. According to Ruud (1994: 2003), the unusual alliance of labourers and landowners also had its roots in a conscious Left Front strategy. When it came to power, the Left Front took care to minimize opposition by ensuring that it did not antagonize all landlords.

Since the 1990s, people's resentment against CPI(M) rule across the state, resulted in the rise of two opposition parties. Trinamul, an opposition group that had split from the Congress party under the leadership of Mamata Banerjee, and for the 2009 parliamentary elections allied with the Congress. The other opposition party is the Hindu nationalist Bharatiya Janata Party which ran the Central Government from 1998-2004. Although CPI(M) rule by no means meant an absence of conflict in West Bengal or in Janta, the growth of the opposition has led to a massive new wave of political turmoil and violence in the state. The number of political murders in Left-ruled West Bengal is highest in the country (*Times of India,* 16 April 2004).

POLITICS AS MORALITY

Two aspects of the local understanding of politics provide a clue as to how the meaning of politics transcends the usual definition of politics as public, goal-oriented work. Parties are expected to get involved in the family affairs of their supporters when necessary and party work is judged according to moral principles. The understanding of politics as morality is in line with the literal meaning of *rajniti* (politics), which is a compound word consisting of the words *raj* (king, ruler, state or government) and *niti* (morality, principle). The following excerpts from interviews with a CPI(M) and a BJP activist illustrate how villagers talk about politics in terms of morality, duties and mutual relationships of service and support:

Phatik Kundu, a BJP activist and large landholder, belongs to the Tili caste:

How many years have you been active in politics (rajniti korechhen)?
Eight years.

Whom did you support first?
At first I supported the Congress, and then CPI(M). CPI(M) oppressed the people, and because of the oppression I now support the BJP.

What do you mean by oppression?
Oppression means that they do not grant people their democratic rights. This causes agitation. Party politics should not be seen only as a means of earning profit, it also entails giving. If one works for a party only to satisfy one's self-interest, in that case the party has become selfish.

What does the BJP want to do? How does it differ from the CPI(M)?
The two differ inherently. We have taken the point of view that we want our democratic rights. The BJP do not create a reign of terror in the villages. They advocate fellow feeling among people. They demonstrate their point of view by doing good work. If somebody acts unjustly, they protest.

What does the BJP want to do for the village?
Many kinds of developments are required: for instance, if there is no school, if there are conflicts [the party intervenes], encouraging [people] to maintain good relationships with one's relatives. The BJP's sense of morality is not the sort that would force people to give up relationships with their *kutum* (in-laws). This is the morality of the CPI(M). Whatever a party does, relationships *(samparko)* between people ought to be good. This is the BJP's morality. The CPI(M) say that one should not visit the house of a BJP supporter. One should not talk to them. You cannot employ any person [from that house]. That is the morality of CPI(M), but not of the BJP. Whatever the relationship is, let it be. Everyone can support the party he or she wants to; it's a democratic right. The CPI(M) say they have given people their rights, but they have not given any rights whatsoever. But the BJP support the idea of democratic rights and say one should maintain one's relationships *(samparko)*.

What kind of problems do you discuss at meetings?
For example, if a poor person gets into trouble, [or] if a poor person falls ill, we take him to a hospital. It's our duty. If somebody cannot arrange a daughter's marriage, everybody helps by contributing [something].

Does the BJP think of women's problems?
Yes it does.

How?
If the husband and wife fight, the dispute will be settled within the village. Husbands and wives should not live in discontent.

I have noticed that here even the rich support the leftist parties.
Yes, for profit. Rich people support the Left Front. They do that to ensure that they do not lose their lands or run into labour problems. They do it out of fear. For example, if somebody has a factory, they do it so that they can run the factory [without interference].

Sunil Bagdi, a CPI(M) activist and a share-cropper belonging to the Bagdi caste:

What do you do for the party? What kind of work?
I do not work for the party. I work for the people.

What have you done?
I offer help *(sohojogita)* of all kinds. If somebody has problems, we have to help.

Do you go to meetings?
Yes, we go to meetings. When they have given us the party schedule, it is our duty *(kortobyo)* [to go to meetings].

Why do you all support this party?
It is for our own benefit. This party works for poor people's benefit. For instance, take the land reform [the poor] are now getting IRDP loans, seeds and seedlings. There are many kinds of work: roads, schools, bridges, Indira houses. CPI(M) considers the poor.

How?
In many ways, I think. They give land to the landless, a house to those who do not have one, such things.

What else?
Whatever is within their capacity. If the demands are excessive, it is not possible. You know that the CPI(M) is a minority [party]. They do what is within their capacity. They help *(sohojogita)*.

Has the Bagdi caste developed much because of the party?
Yes. The Bagdis and the Bauris, i.e. the daily labourers have benefited. The party has done good deeds for them and is still doing so.

Have you received any training from the party?
We have to go through party courses. They teach us how to behave,

the kind of duties that we have [to do] currently.

What kind of development is needed in the village now?
There are still great problems. You have seen everything and know that there are still big problems. I mean, without the party's work many people would not have food to eat.

Yes.
Many people do not have housing or their roofs are leaking.

People cannot get work every day.
Yes. Work is not always available.

How were the daily labourers able to raise their wages?
The payments were raised through the movement, *andolon*, the strike.

When was this?
The strikes take place every year . . . Those [of us] who work in other people's houses go on strike once a year. Suppose we say that we need Rs.48 for a day's work and they do not agree, we can strike work for one or two days. Even when the farmers agree with us, we call a strike for tradition's sake. They may not give the same amount in another place. They may give less. That is why we have to go on strike, for example, on May Day.

The BJP thinks only about the rich people's interests. For instance, the price of diesel has gone up to benefit shop owners. They are helping the rich. Another example is that this government brought down the price of colour TVs and washing machines. How do we benefit from that? It means that the government is thinking about the rich people.

Do you think that the CPI(M) considers women's problems?
Yes. They consider women's problems. They gave women [representative] quotas [in local government]. We also have the women's committee. Our party says that one third of the seats

should be reserved for women, but the BJP still have not applied this rule.

Both the CPI(M) and the BJP understand good morality as the maintenance of just relationships or, in other words, mutually supportive relationships between the party and its supporters. Party members are supposed to show solidarity with one another and people expect help and support from the party.

When there are irreconcilable disputes in a family such as fights between husbands and wives or between in-laws, the family members can call on party leaders to settle the matter. During my fieldwork I witnessed party members trying to curb excessive gambling and drinking by reprimanding men with addictions. Divorces were rare in the village, but the few cases that I witnessed were settled with the help of the CPI(M) party. The girl's parents seek help from the party, especially to ensure that the groom's family returns at least part of the cash that was paid as a dowry when the marriage was arranged. The party, for example, took an active role in the first divorce case among the Tilis of the village: a Tili woman had decided to get divorced shortly after the marriage after discovering that the groom was mentally handicapped. The party not only helped the girl's family to retrieve most of the dowry, but was also ready to contribute money in order to arrange the girl's second marriage. This would have been the first case of remarriage among the Tilis, and it was probable that a much larger dowry would have to be paid the second time. The CPI(M) had also offered to build a separate house for the young woman, next to that of her parents, where she could live on her own.

If any of its supporters find himself or herself in dire economic straits, the CPI(M) can hand out paddy or seeds for cultivation to help him get by without having to sell his land. The party also helps in cases of serious illnesses that the local public health care system is unable to treat. The state-run health centre (located in one of the nearby villages) does not have many resources and cannot do much beyond carrying out female sterilizations and giving vaccinations. For most ailments villagers consult the self-taught village doctors, which is cheaper than turning to formally educated medical practitioners–general practitioners and specialists in Vishnupur or other towns. In cases of serious illnesses villagers do go to specialists–often the village doctors refer patients whom they cannot help to specialists. The CPI(M) party officials accompany patients to hospitals to ensure that they get admitted. The party connection is especially helpful in getting patients admitted to state hospitals, known to be party strongholds. The party can also give financial aid to pay for lodging expenses incurred by the family which has to stay nearby when the patient is admitted.

The party had tried to raise money for a forty-two-year-old Bagdi man's valve replacement operation, but found the cost, Rs.150,000, far beyond its fund-raising capacity. After returning to Finland, I wrote to Dr. Devi Shetty requesting if he could help arrange the man's treatment, and Dr. Shetty agreed to operate on Ajit Bagdi at his charity clinic in Bangalore. I wrote to the village about his offer and suggested that the party help take the patient to Bangalore. After returning to the village I found out that the party had indeed discussed the case with Dr. Shetty, agreeing to collect money for Shetty's foundation in return for the operation. The party carried out a large-scale collection drive, raising Rs.30000 for the charity foundation, and two party representatives accompanied Ajit Bagdi to Bangalore. The operation was successful. The surgeons replaced the crucial valve with the patient's own tissue (his heart's secondary valve), so he did not need any expensive, long-term medication.

When I returned to the village after the operation, I was received even more warmly than earlier. I was the recipient of collective gratitude from all castes and not only by the people of Janta, but also those of the nearby villages. The surgery helped boost the CPI(M)'s public image and the party used the incident, most vigorously, while campaigning. I managed to be on good terms with all the political parties but helping Ajit Bagdi changed my relationship with the CPI(M). Earlier I had gone to meet the party's representatives to obtain interviews, but now they came to meet me to express their gratitude and find out if there were other ways of helping more patients. I had become their ally, and could not help feeling like one of the comrades.

It is understandable that the landless and the marginal farmers support the party, hoping that the party would see them through hard times, especially during medical emergencies as they are unable to afford the high costs of seeing a specialist or an operation. The CPI(M) have, paradoxically, been able to turn the inadequate health infrastructure into an advantage by using it to gain supporters. Although the party officials and representatives genuinely want to help the seriously ill, the medical system, which depends on personal political patronage, is far from flawless. The local political leaders and organizations may be able to ensure initial visits to specialists but they cannot take care of patients with prolonged illnesses and those who require frequent visits to specialists.

The party organization is a hierarchical system, much like a family, and the top level of the local party organization is expected to act as a patron of its followers. Since most party leaders and activists come from wealthy families, politics entails 'low class people' *(chotto lok)* seeking the help and patronage provided by important men ('influential/wealthy people', *boro lok).*

Despite their shared emphasis on politics as a moral activity and on the patronage relationship, the CPI(M) and BJP activists understand their patron position differently and set different priorities and goals for development. In addition to opposing the CPI(M) leaders and by focusing on their malpractice in disputes, the BJP supporters share an agenda to develop communication systems: to provide the village with electricity, working phone connections, and better roads. The CPI(M) leader and supporters expect broad social reforms to uplift the party's landless labourers. For example, the local CPI(M) leader, who belongs to the Tili caste, mentioned the need for a pension system, while a Bagdi activist spoke of improvement of housing conditions and that minimum wages be kept on a par with the rising cost of living.

The Tili landowners' role in the agricultural workers' union supports Ruud's argument (1994; 2003) about the Left Front as a new forum of negotiation of patron-client relationships. The new element in the relationship is that the landless low caste workers say that they can now negotiate from a new position of power and honour. A comment by a Bagdi union activist (a female activist in a brick workers' union) exemplifies the labourers' new ethos: 'The union is fighting superbly, they are running the movement *(andolan kora)*. We have their support. Whatever we say, they listen. We are not afraid of the bosses. We can tell them clearly: we can work this much, for which you have to pay us this amount.' According to Bagdi activists, peasant leaders make an effort to understand and listen to the workers. In turn, the union peasant leader explained the problems and aspirations of the village's poorest strata at length.

As Ruud (2003) argues, the Left Front peasant leaders were able to mobilize the workers because they were different from an old village head or zamindar to whom the workers were tied for a lifetime by their indebtedness, and in whose presence they did not have courage to raise their voices. This does not imply that the coercive element of the patron-client relationship has completely disappeared. In order to build party offices and run its activities, the CPI(M) relies heavily on its supporters' voluntary work; and it often does not give its supporters the option to not donate or help when asked. On the days that the party collected rice from farmers as donation, villagers referred to the party as a zamindar. Many a villager has become a party activist, dedicating his/her time to collecting donations and attending meetings, because having helped him/her, the party demanded reciprocity.

PARTY KINSHIP

The current opposition parties' criticism of the ruling party is very similar to the CPI(M)'s of the Congress, when the latter was ruling the state.The ruling party is accused of ruling by force and exploiting its position for selfish ends. CPI(M) activists have tried to subdue the escalating opposition throughout the state of West

Bengal through sheer violence. In Janta, too, CPI(M) activists attacked and beat up BJP supporters in order to scare the villagers away from the BJP. Village heads and zamindars have, traditionally, used force to ensure obedience; and neither was this rare within families: elder brothers, husbands, and mothers-in-law could simply beat up family members to make them obey them. However, beatings are only rarely accepted publicly, and often the use of force feeds the spirit of resistance, rather than subduing it. Similarly, violence towards the new opposition seems to have strengthened its spirit. Coercion represents one form of the enactment of power, but it is not the most prominent, widely accepted, or a particularly effective means.

Calling one's political rivals selfish is an effective accusation to which people can easily relate. This accusation is regularly heard in joint families where a family member, whether a man or woman, who does less work than the others, is strongly criticized as 'selfish'. A man who does not contribute his earnings to the joint family is similarly criticized. There is no justification for men to indulge in private expenses; this either leads to disciplinary action, or signals the beginning of a joint family's breaking up into nuclear households.

Political discourse parallels that of kinship morality and the political parties' demand for justice means that the parties are expected to conform to kinship ideals. Changes in political affiliation and fissures among party members have to do with serious insults and outright breach of kinship solidarity between party members. A woman whose honour was maligned by a local CPI(M) leader demanded that the party punish the offender for 'insulting a party brother's wife'. Since the party did not take any action, she transferred her support to the BJP in a public announcement and forbade her husband to go to CPI(M) meetings–and he obeyed. The stabbing incident mentioned earlier was labelled political because it involved the kinship ties of the local CPI(M) leader. As mentioned before, the two men–the victim and the murder suspect–were cousins. The suspect's natal family was criticized for receiving more than its legal share of the joint property. Both men supported the Left Front, and the victim's wife was elected to the panchayat as the Left Front's representative. The suspect, the wealthiest man of the village and a CPI(M) leader, had therefore stabbed his party and cousin. The victim's family was devastated, whereas his political family saw its opportunity. The BJP held a public meeting in the village after which almost the entire Tili neighbourhood changed its affiliation from the CPI(M) to the BJP. Even the victim's wife, who officially represented the Left Front in the panchayat, was now said to represent the BJP in her heart.

The closest Bengali word for a relative is *atmio* (a person with whom one shares something) (Fruzzetti and Östör 1976), and incidents such as the one just mentioned illustrate how party members are also understood to be relatives. Kinship forms the metaphor for the party and its activities so that kinship-based party membership is differentiated from other types of relations, defined on the basis of the indigenous ideas of blood relations, code of conduct, sentiment, and according to spatial aspects. Kinship ties mean certain expectations of solidarity. Serious disagreements about these solidarities can lead to the splitting of the joint family, or termination of interaction among certain kin. Since party members are party brothers, conflicts are inevitable as they are between blood-related brothers. As an informant stated, 'Big parties, like large families, do not stay together.' Brothers should not fight, but they do, and this explains the political factionalism in the village.

Although political relatives resemble other types of relatives in a moral sense, there are also crucial differences. Party membership is, after all, less arbitrary than kinship: one cannot select new blood relatives or *kutum* (relatives through marriage) the way one can change one's political affiliation—especially now that a viable opposition to the ruling party has emerged after decades of Left Front rule. Party membership also cuts across caste, but cross-caste alliances are understood through patron-client behaviour rather than through mere kinship. The low caste informants evaluated their party affiliations in terms of the party's ability to help, whereas the upper castes focused on disputes about honour and kinship obligations.

Political kinship draws on the idioms of kinship, but does not equal other forms of kinship. Kinship and party membership overlap, creating conflicting solidarities. When I mentioned that the communist parties in East Europe had faced resistance when they tried to abolish religion, depriving people of their right to practice religion, the villagers drew an analogy with the Left Front's attempts to deprive party members of their relationship with in-laws *(kutum)* who do not support the Left Front. The BJP activist in the village emphasized that his party, unlike the CPI(M), would allow people to maintain their *somporko* (relationships). I asked the BJP supporter how he related to his brother who supported the CPI(M). He replied he had told his brother they could be on good terms, but he would not be able to help the brother if he got into trouble.

It is the overlap between party membership and kinship that allows parties to be efficient, but also makes politics a vulnerable and conflict-ridden business. National party organizations intervene and consolidate their power by expanding and aggravating local family disputes, and not only by mobilizing their supporters from outside the village, but also by arming them with bombs and guns. Local politics in Janta is, by its cultural definition, burdened by conflicting loyalties and unforeseeable connections between the local and national. No wonder most villagers also characterize politics as trouble *(gondogol)*.

INTERPRETING FACTIONALISM

Perplexingly, the political disputes in the village bear some resemblance to the political processes characterized by Evans-Pritchard (1940) and Fortes (1945) as the fission and fusion in the lineage model as well as to the notion introduced by the critics of the lineage mode: factionalism. As in the fission and fusion of the lineage mode, a political conflict between two people in Janta involves their kinship ties, and the severing of a tie as a result of a dispute activates other ties of solidarity. Lineage theorists did not write about India, but their analyses capture the social morphology of the conflicts in Janta. The obvious complication when applying a lineage model to what goes on in Janta, is that party affiliation itself is considered a form of kinship.

Scholars applying the concept of faction sought to deal with conflicts, change, and individual choice, emphasizing that political processes are rarely entirely dominated by kinship. Although there are various definitions of the concept of faction, factions usually refer to informal, spontaneous, leader-follower groups organized for a particular purpose and which disband when that purpose has been accomplished. Most works on rural politics in India utilize the notion of factionalism. Even Dumont (1970: 164), who tended to reduce all social phenomena in India to the caste hierarchy, remarks that the village factions as an empirical fact do not originate from any traditional principle. The disputes in Janta bear a resemblance to factionalism in that they divide villagers, who then seek patronage from different leaders. Faction is also the word that comes to mind when one tries to account for the political incidents, because the villagers themselves talk about politics in terms *(bhag, daladali)* which appear to correspond to the words 'faction' and 'factionalism'.

However, researchers employing the concept of faction have not used it with reference to folk models, but have sought to delineate universal social processes much along the line that lineage theorists (Evans-Pritchard 1940; Fortes 1946) did. The following excerpt from Nicholas (1966: 51), who studied factionalism in rural India, exemplifies the connection between factional analysis and the structuralism of lineage theorists:

> But, perhaps, once we have a clear idea of the arrangement of parts in Nuer society, we are ready to examine the fine structure of the parts. Now that the Newtonian principles of classical structuralism are known (if indeed they are), we are prepared to have a look at the structure of the atoms and molecules of the social universe. I think we may find that the elementary components of

> the fine structure are in constant motion, and that they are related to one another by different principles than are the parts of a classical social structure . . . At what point of structural analysis should account be taken of factions?

Scholars have sought for a general definition of factions, but in retrospect many of their definitions appear to have described historically specific forms of factionalism. When local elections in India did not feature political parties, factions appeared and were defined as being outside the realm of parties. Bailey (1990), who studied village politics in Orissa, identifies factions as distinct from moral political groups: factions lack a shared ideology and are recruited by a leader with whom the group has only a transactional relationship. The group supports the leader in the hope of getting favours from him. Bailey also noted how political allegiance to factions was compounded by fictional kinship ties. He explained this inconsistency between his observations and the definition of faction by defining factions and moral political groups as ideal types that, in actual life, can appear in combination.

Factionalism continues in rural politics in India but it does so contrary to many earlier definitions of factions. Firstly, factional disputes in Janta are short-term, but they entail a moral aspect: disputes arise when somebody violates the kinship-related code of conduct between party relatives. Transactional relationships between leaders and followers are not judged merely on material grounds, but on the leaders' ability to act as patrons of their followers. Secondly, the introduction of party-oriented elections in rural India has brought party rivalries into factionalism. As my examples from Janta illustrate, parties take sides in disputes and participate in factional conflicts. Short-term factional disputes can be made to serve a party's long-term interests.

Both the faction and lineage approaches have neglected the symbolism of local categories without which it is impossible to understand the domain of politics in Janta. The villager's comment that, 'Parties, like big families, do not stay together', points to the heart of the question of factionalism. It is the symbolic meanings of kinship and patron-client relationships that offer a framework of how the villagers perceive and practise politics. In other words, it is not only about how groups of solidarity dissolve and form again, but also how villagers strive and fight for change—taking up issues that are self-evidently considered political and those that get drawn into political debates.

As Hardiman (1999) points out, another problem with the faction concept has been its preoccupation with vertical ties which link the lowest to the highest at the expense of examining the ties of solidarity within groups sharing the same hierarchical position. This is also true of the conceptualization of politics in Bengal as patron-client ties. Hardiman argues that the research on factions has neglected to examine class solidarity as the basis of political organization. The fact that the wealthy landowners not only joined the Left Front movement but also led it is the most obvious proof refuting the interpretation of the Left Front in West Bengal as a movement by workers and a class unto themselves. Ruud (1994; 2003) calls the relationship between the landowners and landless within the CPI(M) a patron-client relationship, whereas Hardiman labels it class collaboration. The political conflicts in Janta illustrate that the villagers indeed do not only depend on vertical ties, but also rely on their horizontal ties, which they discuss in terms of caste and kinship—not class. Class remains relevant, however: low caste villagers who rely on daily labour have different political goals from those of the landowners. In other words, the salience of caste and kinship identities does not exclude an awareness of common class interests, especially when class and caste identities overlap as they do in Janta. Kinship and caste do not form a separate domain from class politics and development ideas; instead, as this and the previous chapter have demonstrated, concepts of personhood are perceived as central to ideas on development, class identities and politics.

It is therefore understandable why the national and state party organizations focus more on providing villagers with support in disputes than teaching them party ideologies. Parties do teach the party activists and officials their ideologies, but even the activists' knowledge of party ideologies remain limited as the following excerpts from interviews indicate. The CPI(M) leader not only mistakenly regards Communism as the main doctrine postulating individual property rights but also credits the Communists with fighting against the British, although the Indian Communists opposed the Congress Party's independence movement (Chaudhari 1996).

> We want people to exercise their democratic right to vote. People [only] agitate against the CPI(M) because of [a few] small incidents. We want to raise people's social awareness. We support Vietnam and Cuba and the leader Lenin who organized the middle farmers of Russia. Many people are waiting for developments such as those that have taken place in West Bengal, for instance in Bihar. Nobody takes the lead there; therefore scientific awareness is slowly increasing. Seventy years ago the people of the Soviet Union started to think about the poor. Society progressed through primitive communism, slavery and capitalism. We communists think that it is our destiny to obtain the five basic [human] rights through human strategy. We forced the British imperialists to leave and now we will build a balanced and healthy society in which people do not oppress one another. There will be no poverty and illiteracy. We will be able to fulfil the five [*sic*] basic needs: education, food, clothing and housing. Our country has great resources, but there is a lack of planning. Capitalist ideas cannot lead to the implementation of new plans, they only encourage people to take loans. Our principle and aim is to work for the poor and we try to develop working class awareness and thereby build a prosperous society . . . In the ideal society people do not oppress one another *(shason thakbe na)*, there will be no deprivation *(banchana)*, property will stay with the people *(manusher sompod manusher hatei thakbe)*.
>
> —CPI(M) leader, Tili

Since the CPI(M) started advocating its industrialization policy rigorously, this leader argues–apparently less convinced of his statements than before–that most farmers give up their land willingly. According to him, industrialization is currently necessary because the party has observed that all over the world industrialized nations are more prosperous than agricultural ones. His reasoning omits to mention that in its earlier policies, the party emphasized that there is a direct link between agriculture's well-being and economic development, which has also been well documented in the development literature.

A BJP leader defines his ideology against foreign influences represented by the CPI(M):

> We consider CPI(M) a foreign party, they do not give the right kind of guidance. The same [wrong] things are happening in every village. Nor do we need to worry whether Marxism or Leninism was successful in the world. In most cases, those who work for the CPI(M) do so in self-interest. It is doubtful whether they really love the party. They are in the CPI(M) for personal gain, for the sake of their own interests, while we want general improvement. If the country's interest is our main consideration, then we [as activists] will not bring our own interest into it–that is why we work for the BJP.

> *What kind of development is needed in the village?*
> Roads, water and electricity. –A BJP leader, Chasa

Village politics is not detached from the larger political organizations, but neither is it completely dictated by them. Crucial to the interaction between local politics and national political ideologies and organizations are the cultural constructs and social formations through which local and national discourses connect. Instead of representing outside forces and ideas, parties gain supporters in the village by feeding into the local concept of politics and the emerging social organization.

The Left Front rule transferred the authority of the great landowners to the new CPI(M) leaders who emerged from the ranks of middle farmers and were able to dominate in village disputes, panchayat politics and the party organization. There were also factional disputes before the emergence of the sizable opposition to the Left Front, but these took place within the Left Front which, in addition to the CPI(M), includes several smaller leftist parties.

The neat convergence between state policies and informal sources of authority disappeared with the emergence of the new opposition. The newly affluent Tili farmers now contest the CPI(M) leaders' authority through disputes about honour and kinship morality. At the same time, the introduction of quotas for women and low castes in panchayats has reduced villagers' dependency on rich farmers and party leaders. Since the major landowners and old-style village heads are no longer able to influence the implementation of the panchayat policies, the impact of state policies in the village is more direct than before. The new panchayat representation and economic opportunities (new job opportunities and the increasing incomes of small and marginal farmers) have contributed to the diminishing power of the dominant caste, the Tilis, and especially the wealthy farmers, including both leaders of the CPI(M) and the BJP. The diminishing power of the dominant caste has, in turn, influenced the authority of the Tili-dominated village meetings. Disputes are rarely settled at village meetings as a consequence, and open conflicts in the village reflect the dispersal of local authority. The police force is not looked upon as an independent source of authority either; even to report a case to the police one has to first contact the communist party officials.

When I returned to Janta in 2003, the BJP opposition still existed in the village, but the CPI(M) had regained some of its earlier support. Initially the opposition had gained the support of almost the entire Tili neighbourhood, but now almost half of the Tilis supported the CPI(M) and half were with the BJP. The CPI(M) had captured an opposition seat in the 2003 panchayat elections. The CPI(M)'s ability to stay in power in the rural areas, while losing its position in many of the cities, shows how the party has based its power on agrarian social relationships. Some of the reasons for the CPI(M)'s long stay in power are, as the critics of Left Front are eager to point out, its use of brute force and its connection to the state machinery, especially the police and land authorities, as well as the party's wealth. However, in Janta the newly formed BJP opposition was able to assert its power without the CPI(M) ever being able to punish the initiators of the revolt. Later many Tilis reverted to supporting the CPI(M)—not because they were threatened with violence to do so, but because the CPI(M) had become active in helping the villagers with their problems. A small landowner family had, for instance, become involved in a dispute because they had not registered the land properly at the time of purchase. They sought help from the CPI(M), shifting loyalty to them from the BJP. The CPI(M) helped them register and keep their land. The CPI(M) is able to help the villagers more efficiently than the opposition parties because it has more resources and better connections to state authorities. Moreover, the CPI(M) has been able to connect its patronage to its policy formulation, while the opposition groups have not been able to formulate and articulate clear policy programmes beyond disagreeing with the CPI(M) and protecting the kinship-related morality in disputes. The so-called factional village politics is not entirely cut off from the parties' long-term interests, as villagers assess parties in terms of their ability to act as patrons of their followers and the forms of patronage depend on party policies. Broad social policies offer parties more extensive means of helping people and are more effective than single acts of help.

The BJP-led revolt in Janta to protest the misconduct of the local CPI(M) leader had decreased the importance of the village's local 'big men', even though the CPI(M) was able to regain some of its earlier support. Instead of talking about 'doing the party', when seeking help from the party, the villagers now talked about 'doing the party panchayat' and instead of the local 'big men', the villagers increasingly turned to the panchayat secretary when in need of help.

When a major fight occurred in the village in 2004, the village leaders were no longer able to settle the matter. The dispute started off when a woman blamed another woman for stealing vegetables. It spread as the two families to which the women belonged happened to be involved in a dispute over the building of a well. The other family opposed their neighbours' building a well too close to their plot. Many meetings were held in the village but the families involved in the dispute did not heed the solutions. offered. A couple injured badly in the fight wanted to accuse the other side of attempted murder. No party supported their case, but there was no one in the village with the authority to persuade them to stop the court process.

At this time the head of the panchayat was a dalit man and Janta's representatives were two dalit women. While the rural society's new strata participated in local decision-making, the women and Scheduled Caste representatives hardly enjoyed the same authority as those who were also Left Front leaders and owners of big plots. Moreover, it takes an exceptionally active representative to have true influence on resource allocation, because panchayats tend to be more involved with the execution of state policies than with their planning. Both the local village 'big men's' loss of authority as well as the new panchayat representatives' and its head's inexperience and status had resulted in a shift of power to the party secretary, who had held the office for the past twenty years. The quotas for the low castes and women in panchayats have decreased the power of village 'big men', but at the same time power has shifted to the party and panchayat officials outside the village. The dispersal of power outside the village is accentuated by the building of the phone networks, thanks to which seeking help from outside the village during conflicts and crises has become easier. These developments do not imply that the new low caste representatives would be unable to have a growing influence on the local governing organs as they learn through their work.

To conclude, my interpretation of the symbolic construction of village politics differs crucially from Davis's analyses (1983). For Davis, the symbolic construction of politics meant that everybody aimed to keep the symbolic structure intact and unchanging. Davis delineated the cultural construct of politics in local terms and concluded by defining the aim of village politics as the upholding and protecting of the dharma, a polity, society and a view of the cosmos arranged according to an inequality premise. According to Davis (ibid: 109), the goal is defined in relation to the religious framework of Hinduism, which posits the natural and moral order of society as divinely given and thus beyond the agency of human change. In Janta, politics is motivated by symbolic structures, yet 'big people' and 'small people' have been able to raise new and differing demands and interpretations of political goals. The local concept of politics gives ground to critical discourses. The low caste labourers are able to draw from the morality of the patron-client relationships in justifying their demands for better living and working conditions. In turn, the newly affluent Tili farmers find justifications for their cause: to build authority from kinship-related moral discourses. Different interest groups share the same concept of politics, which makes the attaining of political goals an ambiguous process, wrought with unintended consequences that become amplified by the connections between the local politics and national political organizations. The local concept of politics does not exclude kinship and the sphere of home. Consequently, this analysis of local politics has opened up a view to understanding the role of gender in politics.

FOUR

The Gender of Politics

My finding that local politics includes the sphere of the home along with gender and kinship contradicts most prior anthropological studies on local politics in rural West Bengal and India. These studies (such as Nicholas 1966; 1998; Davis 1983; Bailey 1990; Lieten 1992; Ruud 2003) have either focused on men's political participation or noted women's non-attendance at village political meetings. Yet, historical records tell of rural women's mass participation in a broad range of political movements (Sen 1985). Bengali peasant women participated in the nationalist movement, in the Tebhaga movement (a sharecroppers' movement to demand a larger share of their produce) in the 1940s, in the Naxalite and the land-grab movements in the 1960s and most recently in the movement against land acquisitions for special economic zones.

Survey-based studies confirm women's increasing participation in politics in rural West Bengal (Kumar and Ghosh 1996; Sen Chaudhuri 1995). Datta (2000) explores all-women panchayats of Maharastra in the 1980s and 1990s, intertwining elements of political studies and feminism. As she notes, a few all-women panchayats are known to have been formed after independence in Karnataka, Orissa, Madhya Pradesh and Maharastra—the first all-woman panchayat was formed in the 1960s in Pune district.

Women were involved in rural politics even at the time anthropological studies noted women's absence from formal politics. The fact that most anthropological studies on rural politics were written by men who do not have the same access to the world of rural women as women do may have contributed to the neglect of women's informal political activities and the gendered nature of politics.

THE NATIONALIST BURDEN OF FEMALE ACTIVISM

Forms of female political activism as recorded in historical archives arose as a response to organized movements in rural Bengal. Women's local action is not completely dictated by these movements, but these institutions–and their colonial history–have shaped women's political participation. Since women's political action in Janta is related to these past patterns of action and discourses, I shall start off by discussing the colonial history of women's movement in India.

The first organizations to mobilize women for political work were founded during the nationalist movement, which shaped women's political activism in Bengal profoundly. Women participated in the nationalist movement by joining processions, wearing *khaddar* (locally made handloom cloth to discourage the buying of British products) and giving shelter to revolutionaries on the run in Calcutta as well as in district towns and villages (Forbes 1999: 135). Forbes (ibid: 123) notes how the women's participation differed from the men's: many of the women's political acts were hidden from the police and the public eye. Women provided cover for revolutionary acts by hiding weapons and fugitives but they also moved to the public sphere. Middle and upper class women, who had previously rarely moved outside their homes, joined public demonstrations. By the 1930s, women became directly involved in revolutionary acts, as in the case of the two college girls who shot and killed Magistrate Stevens (ibid: 140). Forbes (ibid: 155) notes how many of the female activists openly espoused feminist ideology, but these goals were set aside for the common good of the nation. The men accepted the women's revolutionary activities as long as they took place under male guardianship and did not upset family life as exemplified by the following incident cited by Forbes (ibid: 121): a husband whose wife had been arrested for her participation in a demonstration found that it was a great honour to have his wife arrested, but expressed his unhappiness that she had not asked his permission to leave the house. The revolutionary female activists interviewed by Forbes recalled that they were motivated to join the nationalist movement because 'the house is on fire and women should come out of the burning house and help put out the fire'; women were expected to go back to the inner chambers after the fire had been extinguished (ibid: 121, 156).

It was not merely women's concrete participation that helped build the nation; women and womanhood also played a crucial symbolic role in the movement against colonialism. The need to reform women had arisen as a response to the British assertion of cultural and moral supremacy, based on their view of Hindu society as degrading women. Mani argues (1998: 117-118) that women were neither the subject nor the object of the Indian debate on the women's question; they were rather the ground and the site on which tradition was debated and reformulated. Rather than challenging the Hindu ideas of womanhood, the nationalist elite's solution to the women's question sought to challenge the British proclaimed supremacy by insisting on protecting and strengthening the true Hindu identity and its repositories: women. Women symbolized the nation and the spiritual quality of the national culture, which had to be preserved and nurtured even if other spheres of life changed (Chatterjee 1993). As Fruzzetti and Perez (2002) demonstrate, women were and are still considered the embodiment and the nurturers of values and tradition.

So far the research on colonial history has paid more attention to women as the objects of colonial discourses than as subjects. Sarkar's (2001) analysis of *Amar Jibon*, the first autobiography written by a Bengali woman, first published in 1868, shows that women's lives were not completely dictated by the colonial discourses. The writer of the autobiography, Rassundari Devi, a housewife from an upper-caste landed family in East Bengal, lived the life that militant Hindu revivalist-nationalists of the nineteenth century had valorized. Yet, as Sarkar illustrates, her autobiography expresses major transgressions, the foremost of which was Rassundari Devi's learning to read and write secretly.

Not all women's organizations carry the nationalist burden, but the nationalist resolution of the women's question has been institutionalized in many of them as Fruzzetti's (2003) research shows. Rather than the creation of alternative gender structures, many women social workers and activists perceive their task as the protection of women. The first efforts to organize Bengal's rural women were made by the Mahila Atmaraksha Samiti, the Women's Self-Protection Society in the aftermath of the great famine. The Mahila Atmaraksha Samiti had evolved from the Congress Mahila Sangha, an organization seeking to teach women to protect themselves if a Japanese invasion should occur. In 1943, the Mahila Atmaraksha Samiti organized demonstrations in several Bengal districts where women protested against the rising prices and demanded food. In Midnapur, women surrounded a rice mill and succeeded in pressurizing the mill owner to sell rice at the price that they wanted to pay. (Forbes 1999: 210)

Rural women's spontaneous action had a prominent role in the Tebhaga movement in the 1940s. This movement was organized by communists who led the sharecroppers demanding to keep two-thirds of the harvest. Sen (1985) cites police records in which women are reported as having marched in processions armed with sticks, overpowering the police by surrounding them, organizing warning systems and offering underground activists shelter during the movement. Women first had an auxiliary role in the movement: they helped harvest the crops, cooked food for the leaders and acted as lookouts. When the police action against the activists turned brutal, the Communist Party, unprepared for an armed struggle, withdrew from active leadership, and the women formed their own militia, the *naribahini*. Female leaders argued for the need to introduce women's issues to the movement's agenda, but the party and the union rejected their suggestions (Forbes 1999: 215). Women were also mobilized in the land-grab movement of the 1960s and in the Naxalite insurgency by a radical Maoist group that broke away from the Communist movement in 1967. Women joined demonstrations and confronted the police when the male activists were in hiding and kept contact with the activists.

The Mahila Atmaraksha Samiti, which had had to go underground when the Communist Party was declared illegal, emerged again as the Paschim Bangla Mahila Samiti (PBMS) in 1953. When the Communist Party split into the CPI and CPI(M), the women's organization followed suit: the PBMS remained affiliated with the CPI, whereas Paschim Bangla Ganatantrik Mahila Samiti (PBGMS) was established as a separate organization linked to the CPI(M) (Basu 1992: 60-61). By the 1950s, all the major parties had their women's fronts and women were always mobilized for demonstrations. But unions and parties, including the CPI(M), have tended to neglect women's interests as, for example, Basu (2002) and Fernandez (1994) have demonstrated. Women continue to be included in political movements as the effective symbols of the inner core of Hindu society rather than as political subjects.

FEMALE FORMS OF POLITICAL ACTIVISM

Even women who are not party activists commonly discuss village politics in Janta and get involved in factional disputes that are labelled political. Incidents and conflicts stimulated by the breaking of the party-related code of conduct and their aftermaths are topics that inspire intense discussions on the morality of parties. As described in Chapter 3, women can choose sides and impose their choice on their household members.

The following incident of women's spontaneous political action resembles the earlier patterns of female activism in rural Bengal in many ways. The local BJP supporters decided to put an end to the harassment and intimidation by the CPI(M) supporters and attacked the CPI(M) leaders who had gathered for a meeting. CPI(M) supporters were able to send word and call for help, and a special police riot unit came to the village to pick up the suspects. BJP leaders called on the Tili women to help and the women responded to their call: 'If the village is on fire, should we not help to put out the fire?' they later asked in explanation. They surrounded the police cars the whole day, effectively preventing the police from picking up the suspects from the village. Afterwards they told me how difficult it had been to engage in holding a day-long siege and cooking at the same time.

In the course of the siege, the women insulted the policemen. A policeman hit a woman with his baton, in retaliation to something she said. By that time the head of police at Bankura had arrived on the scene and reprimanded the concerned policeman, thanking the villagers for keeping calm. The women thereafter made tea for the police who then left—without having arrested the suspected rioters.

Women repeatedly reminded me to write about the siege. They are proud of the incident and with reason: they were able to save Tili men by their action, and at the same time demonstrate their power and fearlessness. When women talk about the incident they emphasize their role in comparison to that of the men 'who helped from the side by giving us courage'. The local male BJP leader merely mentioned that the village women had helped them to teach the communists a lesson without going into the details of the incident. These differing gendered narratives are another reminder of how incomplete accounts and stories are. Although the BJP activist clearly plays down the women's role, he is partly right: the women's siege was not an autonomous rising; they acted when the local BJP activists who had been in trouble called them to do so. Some of the women who are known for their open defence of women's rights came to defend the BJP—many of whose male activists are known to assert that women's place is in the home. Yet, the women's actions gave the men an idea of the power possessed by the women.

Women's activism was related to men's activities, but the

women acted separately, not simultaneously or together with the men: the women moved into the limelight to resist the police after men had beaten their opponents and moved to the background. Similarly, the CPI(M), which organizes women into *mahila samitis* (women's committees), follows a pattern of separate action for women. Women are not excluded from politics, but participate separately from men. This division parallels the symbolic structure that Fruzzetti (1990) found in her study of marriage rituals in Bengali Hindu society. She concludes that women are both encompassed by and complementary to men in the concept of the person, the construction of caste-kinship groups, the indigenous understanding of hierarchy, and the idea of male/female relatedness. Family disputes, along with women's demands, are readily understood as political because politics in Bengal is not perceived in opposition to the women's domain of household and kinship as has been the case in societies where western ideas of politics have evolved. Rajniti is the domain of the ruler's morality, guided by the interrelated meanings of gender, kinship, and patron-client relationships.

Without prior experience of confronting the police, Tili women resorted to the same pattern of action as women in the political movements of the past had done—confronting the police by surrounding them and acting in an auxiliary role to that of men—which proves the existence of an enduring conceptualization of women's role in political action—a folklore of women rioting in rural Bengal. As in the organized movements of the past, women were employed by the party for their ability to defend the common good and not to pursue their own goals. The women of Janta used the exact same words, 'Women have to come out to put out the fire' like the female revolutionaries of the nationalist movement (as cited by Forbes 1999) to justify their action. They did not leave their houses to challenge their cultural code of conduct, but as ideal women to defend the common good. In defending the men of their neighborhood, women joined the protest against the unjust deeds of the CPI(M), consequently protecting the kinship-related code of conduct and morality. The motivation of the local BJP in mobilizing women and the women's motivation for surrounding the police cars both build on the idea of women as the embodiment and protectors of the society, not that of the nation, but of the village and the caste neighbourhood. The nationalist resolution of the women's question conforms well to the village understanding of politics and may even have strengthened the vision of women as the protectors of their society in rural Bengal, because it has motivated political organizations to employ the idea of women as the embodiment of society when mobilizing them.

The majority of women do not only participate in spontaneous politics. Of the forty-four women I interviewed in Janta on their voting pattern, forty-three said they voted according to their own preference. (One woman said she took her sons' advice regarding whom to vote for.) The Left Front rule has introduced two political arenas for rural women: mahila samiti and panchayats (village councils). Mahila samitis, which the CPI(M) set up in the 1970s and 1980s, have been credited with giving peasant women perceptions of dignity and for involving them in child welfare, informal education, and for setting up craft centres–and criticized for not challenging the prescribed gender code of conduct and the concomitant restrictions (Basu 1992).

According to Tapati Kundu, a mahila samiti activist, women's informal collective action in the villages may be even more common and extensive than that of CPI(M) organized mahila samitis. 'Women who live next to each other go to the police station and protest against harassment. This happens in every village. But there are no formal mahila samitis in all villages. They are there informally, but I do not see a women's committee with women attending a meeting every week or every month in every village,' she says. Consequently, the success of mahila samitis depends on their ability to connect with and provide an avenue for women's spontaneous political action.

Nevertheless, mahila samitis have become such a routine phenomenon in Bankura district that the male officers of the district CPI(M) office expressed disbelief when I told them that women in my home country, Finland, are not as extensively organized. The district level organization of the women's committee is responsible for setting up the committees and drawing general outlines of the local committees' activities. Because of the difficulty of finding suitable leaders, not all committees are equally active and even the active ones may see a lull.

Janta's women's committee is involved in setting up income earning opportunities and adult education classes for women, solving family disputes and fights and making women conscious of their rights. In 2003, the women's committees started to set up self-help groups under a panchayat scheme found throughout rural West Bengal. The groups have two major functions: mutual support and micro-credit. In return for their monthly saving of Rs.10, each woman consecutively obtains a lump sum as a loan. Women also take turns to act as an advisor to others. Information on health issues and a healthy diet is, for example, given to the groups. During my stay in the village the first batch of women received loans and invested them in such activities as cultivation, buying of domestic animals, starting a popped rice (muri) business and some lent the money at a higher interest rate to other business initiatives. Each woman was able to pay back the amount loaned to her. Although the amount of credit was small at this stage (a few thousand rupees), the recipients were quite enthusiastic and aware of the prospect of getting larger loans in future and found managing the credit system an empowering experience.

As with general village meetings, disputes may be solved and the guilty party fined at mahila samiti meetings. In case of a woman being mistreated by her family, committee representatives can discuss the situation with the family to look for a solution. The mere threat of the committee's involvement may motivate family members to refrain from mistreating a woman. Nevertheless, in its settlement of a dispute, an important goal of the women's committee is to protect the kinship-related code of conduct, such as the sanctity of marriage. The committee, for example, solved the problem of a man having an extramarital affair by deciding that the man, after having married the second woman, should share his time with both wives equitably. The first wife did not, however, accept this solution and left the village.

Village riots in Janta made the situation too explosive for regular women's meetings. The mahila samiti affiliated with the Left Front lost its major source of support when the majority of the Tili neighbourhood switched their political affiliation to the BJP. Although local BJP leaders spoke of the need to set up their own women's committee in the village, it seemed unlikely that it could accomplish as much as the CPI(M)-run women's committee. The local BJP activists differed in their opinion on women's mobilization: one was in favour of setting up a women's committee along the principles of the Left Front-organized committees, another did not believe that women could have any public role and the third merely understood women's issues as the need to solve family conflicts. No BJP-led organization has actually mobilized women separately from men in the region. The women recognized the benefits they received from the Left Front and one activist, who had shifted her support to the BJP, even told me that she was planning to switch back to the Left Front later as it offered greater resources for women.

As it was the village panchayat representative who founded the mahila samiti in Janta, the panchayat programmes for women have been closely associated with it. The mahila samiti focuses on raising women's consciousness about their rights, but it may also motivate women to participate in programmes as well as the panchayat to pay attention to their concerns. Depending on their willingness and ability, women representatives can introduce and set up new programmes for other women. Tapati Kundu helped facilitate income-generating opportunities, run a female literacy programme and a nursery school in Janta. Although the panchayat may limit its action to the implementation of government-planned programmes, women panchayat representatives matter to rural women as they help them get funds. Women in need of assistance find it easier to approach female representatives. Rekha Bose, who runs the mahila samitis in the panchayat to which Janta belongs and who has also served a five-year term as the head of the panchayat, relates her experiences:

> Women are happy to tell me about their problems when I visit them. Women find it difficult to open up in front of male-dominated administrative units. When I was the head of the panchayat, women came forward. I would ask them about their desires and needs, such as the availability of drinking water and health care. Sometimes they want to learn a vocational skill. If women have some income, the family situation improves.

Women panchayat representatives are commonly criticized for acting as the mouthpiece of the men in their families as most of them come from families where men have been politically active. Of the twelve all-women panchayats analysed by Datta (2000), nine worked well while the rest were influenced by men's interests. As cited by Rai et al. (2001), a study (PRIA 1999) on women's leadership in the panchayats of six states shows that the most important information source for female panchayat members is their immediate male family members. Rai et al. (ibid.) describe the case of a female head of panchayat in Uttar Pradesh serving as a proxy for her husband: the woman pradhan (the head of the panchayat) did not attend a single meeting and the villagers called her husband the head of the panchayat. Basu (1992: 69) observed that the female panchayat members in rural Midnapur district of West Bengal tended to be more reticent than the male members in expressing their views during panchayat deliberations.

However, female activists' family background need not only be an obstacle. The family and its male members can support a woman's public role rather than preventing her from making her own decisions. In their evaluation of panchayat reform in India, Rai et al. (2001) describe both women's difficulties in gaining legitimacy in the political sphere as well as cases of successful female representatives such as Shimburi Devi of the

Alwar district in Rajasthan. The women of her village had sought her help, and she was able to stop the selling of illicit liquor in the village by having the women surround the shop after the police had ignored her requests to close it.

Yet, women representatives' work is often hindered and their morality questioned because they move outside the conventional female sphere. Women's participation may also be obstructed by their lack of experience and skill, although they can overcome such obstacles, as Rumme Bai from the Seoni district in Madhya Pradesh did. After overcoming her own feelings of helplessness, she raised village issues, especially those concerning women, at the meetings. Her work gained her the people's confidence, but since she stayed out late, attending evening meetings, gossip was circulated about her. Her family and husband supported her despite the controversy, and the community, though they had differing opinions about her, appreciated her work. (Rai et al. 114-121)

Of the twelve all-women panchayats studied by Datta (2000), nine were formed and run by women and three were formed at the behest of men, e.g. by a sugar baron who used women's panchayat to maintain his hold on local politics, by village men who wanted to avoid factions by appointing a women's panchayat that they could control and by male activists who wanted to support the call for rural women to enter into politics. However, according to Datta, even panchayats started by women's initiatives received indirect or direct support from the male leaders. She concludes that all-women panchayats were most effective in solving issues such as water scarcity which did not directly challenge men's power. Nevertheless, women's entry into politics led to changes in the power dynamics between the sexes. The most visible example was a female panchayat leader whose new political position led to a visible change in her family status: her husband stopped battering her and her health improved.

Women's political participation draws from the local concept of politics that allows women a role as long as their agenda follows the local understanding of politics as the protection of the kinship-related code of gendered conduct. However, some political activities—such as attending public meetings outside the village—do not strictly conform to the cultural code of conduct for village women. Moreover, women's agenda may at times be directed towards changing the expected cultural code of conduct.

I will next examine the work and ideologies of Janta's female activists (two panchayat representatives and a union activist) as well as those of a few from the surrounding region (a secretary of the mahila samiti's district council from Vishnupur, a mahila samiti activist from Udbastukendra village and a former head of the panchayat and mahila samiti activist from Gora village). The question at this point is: do female activists strive to reproduce or change the cultural code of conduct for women and do they share an ideology?

ACTIVIST IDEOLOGIES

The activists emphasized the importance of women's awakening, of women becoming conscious of their shared situation. Through their ideas and the process of awakening, female activists separate the active consciousness from the taken-for-granted form of consciousness. J. and J. Comaroff (1991) have called the former ideology and the latter hegemony, and I will adopt their usage of the terms, albeit in a different sense and context. Comaroff and Comaroff's definition of ideology interestingly follows the female activists' own understanding of their awakening. My analysis is accompanied by lengthy excerpts from female activists' own accounts because I want to offer the reader a chance to grasp the women's thinking in their own words as well as through my interpretations—the reader can also choose to skip either part.

By the fall of 2003 four women in total represented Janta in the panchayat. The two new low caste representatives had just started their term and were therefore not able to discuss their experiences when I was in the village. I will examine how the former female representatives, Jharna Kundu and Tapati Kundu, view their experiences. Both women belong to families with political authority in the village and both were living in their parents' village at the time of their panchayat term. Tapati Kundu was unmarried during her panchayat term, while Jharna Kundu's parents had arranged her marriage in the same village as they wanted to have one daughter stay near them. Not all female representatives live in their natal villages (Janta's two new representatives live with their in-laws), although the general belief is that women living in their natal villages are freer to participate in formal politics than women living in their in-laws' village, as most married women do. Jharna Kundu's brother-in-law is a CPI(M) leader and one of the richest men of the village. The family of Tapati Kundu's father had once owned the largest amount of land in the village. Her father and grandfather have both represented the village in the local governing bodies.

The Left Front activists appealed to the traditional methods of dispute settlement by suggesting that no female candidate should disgrace herself by contesting Tapati Kundu's candidature–village disputes are usually informally solved by unanimous decisions. Nevertheless, a Congress party candidate stood against her and lost. Tapati Kundu joined the panchayat at her father's suggestion and she emphasizes her father's influence on her entry into politics. Yet, as her own account of the development of her work and thinking reflects, her main goal has not been to follow her father's orders but to work for women:

> There were six or seven of us, women. We always discussed the work together. We did not discuss things with men much. Why should we depend on men? We tried getting money for women. If I alone objected to something or said something in the panchayat, nobody would listen to me. So, I used to consult other women. If I could not get them all together, I gathered some of them and we surrounded *(gherao)* the development block office to obtain our rights. And when I didn't like some decision taken by the panchayat office, I told them: you have to give me this or we women will be excluded from [the panchayat]. I demanded things for people who had lost their houses and clothes in the floods, did not have winter

clothes, those whose roofs leaked during the monsoon season or who had no roof over their heads. I used to help [those who needed it] get clothes, wheat and paddy from the Block Development Office. I helped those who did not have money for a son's education, were old, disowned by their husband or were widowed. I helped them obtain funding. I used to send those who had failed to get money even after having applied for the second time to the district council. Again, if I did not get help for the women of our society, I used to go to the district council. I also arranged funding for installing deep tube wells.

I want to say that when I passed the Higher Secondary Exam, I wanted to do something. I did not want to sit idle in the least. . . . I always thought about women. My father always thought about helping women to progress. He wanted us to at least know the wrongs of the society . . . and showed the way to fight for our rights. He helped us in every way to get an education [and] . . . introduced us to many things . . . I thought that I would do something for the advancement of society. My father encouraged me to take a six-month course on women and children. Almost 3500 women were interviewed for this course . . . and I . . . was admitted to the training.

I went to a remote village called Khirindaa. Of the seventy-five women in our group, some were from villages and some from cities. I noticed that many women were advanced and there was so much to learn from them. They said, 'Why should we be beaten by men? Why shouldn't we protest? Why cannot women who get beaten up by their husbands divorce? Why should children be hungry and wash cups in tea stalls?'

I understood that there had been an awakening *(jagaron)* in their minds. So after finishing the training and returning to village, I immediately protested *(pratibad)* if I saw a man doing anything wrong. I immediately protested whenever a man or an uncle *(kaka or jetha)* beat his wife. I said, 'I will call a meeting of the party, make you ask your wife for forgiveness and pay a fine.' To do this I had to organize a mahila samiti. I arranged a meeting for women and explained many things to them. I said, 'It's wrong to have your child sit idly at home. I have opened a children's centre. Send him/her there. Why do you accept the given situation? Do some work. Fry muri, boil rice and sell that. Why is your land lying waste? You cannot just remain a housewife. If men do not work, women have to go out in the fields. Raising a child does not mean just giving him food and clothes, you have to educate him. You have to make him useful for society. Our village is underdeveloped. You have not lived in a city; you have not been to other developed villages. You have no idea how far behind we are.'

Many women from Bagdi para, at least forty-five to fifty, would come to study in my primary school. I not only taught them to read and write, but also would talk about how women should be awakened, how they should progress, what could be done for their well-being and for their children and what they could do to keep their husbands healthy. I used to focus on the different problems faced by women. At that time all literacy programme centres asked me [to speak].

I was a member of the RSP (Revolutionary Socialist Party), and formed the mahila samiti . . . the meetings at the school [were] about women and children [and] had nothing to do with the party. There were people with different ideas, from different parties. Why would they respond to the RSP's call? I tried to convince them that those who were interested could go to the district meetings. If I could take a few women there, they could return to tell others what was going on. We try to say, 'Women should move forward, they should not stay behind, they should support themselves, they have to earn. Women and men are equal. Don't look down upon women. A daughter is the same as a son. It isn't only a son who keeps a family line alive, a daughter does the same. A daughter is your child as is your son. So don't love only your son, love your daughter too.'

What is the main problem for women here?

The main problem for our women is the dowry [system]. Women have to be given away for marriage and therefore they are neglected.

'We have to pay for your marriage, so don't ask for good clothes, jewellery and good food now. Where will I find [money for] this? I have to give so much money for your marriage. Where will I get this? We [will] have to sell our land.'

No, it does not stop. It has come to such an extreme that the groom's family, which takes a dowry at the time of marriage, wants more afterwards and punishes the bride if the woman's family fails to give more jewellery.

Women [also] commit suicide. It happens if the woman's family is unable to give a dowry. Some women hang themselves. Some families poison their daughters-in-law or hang her [and] hide their crimes. Now we are told that our Constitution forbids dowry. Offering and taking dowry are both considered offences, but rich people say that they want to give their daughters gifts, not a dowry. As a result even those who cannot afford to give a dowry are compelled to do so. Grooms' parents say, 'Whatever you give is meant for your daughter, after all.' They demand this and no one considers it illegal. People do not follow the law. I now work in Samaj Kalyan Daptar for women and children's welfare. We hold meetings with women. I tell them, 'You can do it. Do not give any gifts on your daughter's marriage. Do not act illegally.' It is true that dowry creates a kind of fear in people's minds, but nothing has changed.

I think [crimes against women] occur more in villages than in cities. Is this because women in the cities have jobs?

Women in cities have jobs. Most men [there] want 'good' [from a good family, with some education and skills] women. If necessary, the groom's family pays a dowry to bring the woman to their home, they give their jewellery to the bride to wear. But a father-in-law, mother-in-law and husband in a village would not do this. The dowry system is practised more commonly.

What other problems do women in a village have? Do many men beat women?

Men used to beat women more in the past, now it is much less.

It has become less?
Now women protest more. They do not accept such behavior.

What do the mahila samitis do for women?
We want to increase women's awareness. We tell them not to accept torture. We make people understand that they can do something. There will be unrest in the family, but women are no less [valuable] than men are. There are rules and regulations regarding women's behaviour in our society. If a woman breaks the rules and does something bad, most men get angry. They beat their wives or harass them. I tell the women, 'Behave properly as far as you can. Try to adjust. If your husband does something bad or does something wrong, try to talk to him, take time and try to bring him around in the right way.' Many women follow this and are doing fine, better than they were before.

Our village has become more developed and young men and women are interested in getting educated. Every family has a gem [a child], because most children pass the school-leaving exams securing first division, go to colleges and universities. They mix with the people from the outside world. When they come back home, they protest, 'This is wrong. This should not be done,' or say, 'It brings shame on us. When our friends visit, they might think that we are uncultured.' The proportion of educated people has risen in the village.

Has anyone objected to the work you have done for women?
There are obstacles to all social work. People tried to stop even Ishwarchandra Vidyasagar. We are ordinary people. No wonder we face opposition. Sometimes, someone might be apparently nice to me, but oppose me behind my back, trying to stop me. But I am never disheartened. I was never afraid of anything. I used to be out with a torch till 11.30 or midnight. Many people noticed me, but I did not know what fear was. But now I am afraid of many things because I feel weaker since childbirth. When I am able to go out again, I will do social work.

Discussions about our society crop up. In our society women

> want to obtain government jobs. Men do not take care of their children. They only know how to have fun. Sometimes we do not get money (from our men) to raise our children, so we should get the jobs. We should be employed in different types of work in our society.
>
> Urban women protest more. My ultimate goal is that we should not make our children suffer. We should give them good clothes, food and education. Mothers can provide these for their children, so why don't women get the jobs? Local government seats are [now] reserved for women because of these demands.
>
> Women and men are equal according to our Constitution, but not in reality. Women themselves are mostly responsible for this. Women are not truly enlightened. Women have to wake up *(jege uthte hobe)*, they have to speak and fight for their rights. Suppose five women in a village have been made aware [of their rights]. If they make five more women conscious, it will happen. If they keep their ideas to themselves, how will women progress? How will they be conscious of their rights? Many women do not express themselves. When ideas enter villages, women become aware *(jagchhe)*.

Tapati Kundu enjoyed an unusual position for a village woman during her term in the panchayat. She, an unmarried college girl, was able to prevent incidents of family violence just by threatening to throw the perpetrators into prison. She was also able to move about in the village alone even after sunset, which Tili women rarely do. Her belonging to a family with a tradition of local authority contributed to her power without turning her into her father's proxy.

Tapati Kundu's activities also exemplify the influence of women's organizations. She emphasizes that it was the training course for women that resulted in her awakening. Like the other women involved in women's organizations whom I interviewed, she believed that women needed to be awakened to be able to express themselves and demand changes.

The interview with Tapati Sardar (a member of the mahila samiti's district council) provides an example of the female activists' understanding of political consciousness:

> *Does CPI(M) think about women?*
> Of course. They think about women's problems, and ways of solving problems.
>
> *The number of women in politics is still less than that of men. Why?*
> It is easier for men to travel to meetings, they can leave the house at any time, but women have to consider the household *(sansar)* responsibilities. In spite of these constraints, women of West Bengal have become conscious and moved forward. The government of West Bengal have several provisions for them and this has increased their consciousness. In West Bengal, as well as the rest of the country, women have become conscious *(sachetan)*.
>
> *How has the government helped women?*
> They have improved the opportunities for women to obtain government jobs. Women can be employed in service *(chakri)* just like men. Women can stand for panchayat elections, 33 per cent of seats are reserved for women. We protest against family problems. Earlier women could not protest, they were beaten; husbands drank and beat their wives. Now women can protest. Husbands now know that what they do is bad. Women have developed this sense. Earlier women had to accept whatever the husband said. It is still like that, but less than before.

Women used the term *jagaron,* which as we saw, literally means awakening or the word *sachetan,* conscious. Marx, followed by Marxist scholars, introduced consciousness raising as the precondition for revolutionary activities; these women hardly proceed to consciousness raising because of the universality of Marxist theories but because they have been influenced by their organizations to think in this way. The second female panchayat representative in Janta, who has not been involved in any feminist-inclined organization, lacks the notion of awakening:

What do you discuss in the meetings?
We discuss a plan of action and where to apply it. What, for example, may be done to support widows, old people and mothers of newborn babies. We also discuss the construction of roads and digging of tube wells.

How many women are there in the panchayat?
There are six to seven.

Do women discuss matters among themselves and separately from the men?
No, we all discuss matters together.

Does the panchayat look after women's interests?
Yes. It looks after women's interests more than men's.

How?
Through family issues *(sansar)*, for instance.

What does the panchayat do for women?
It has a health programme for women, telling them how convenient it is to have small families [so that] one can raise children well, keep them healthy and cure illnesses easily. They have also facilitated the treatment of women patients in the hospitals.

What kind of development (unnoti) should there be for women?
The development needed in women's lives is that they should be able to have small families and live in peace.

Do all parties take women's problems into consideration?
Yes. All parties do.

What is the difference between the BJP and RSP?
There is no difference when it comes to meetings, although there is a difference between the parties in the village. At meetings everyone wants progress (to move forward, *egoy*). No one speaks ill of anyone, they express the party's point of view.

Not so many women are actively involved in politics. Why do you think it is so?
Women do not have the courage. Now everyone has some education.

Jharna Kundu perceives women's agenda as providing healthcare and family planning services and the panchayat as the executioner of government-planned programmes, to a degree that she views panchayat to be outside the realm of local political contests and the disputes. She also equates women's concerns with issues of family welfare. Unlike Tapati Kundu, Jharna was not supported by her politically powerful relatives: her husband's murder had turned her and the entire Tili neighbourhood against her powerful brother-in-law.

According to Tapati Kundu, awakening means that women should identify and protest against cultural practices that are harmful to them. This entails both protesting against breaches of the kinship-related code of conduct and demanding changes in cultural practices, such as the marriage system. She advocates the protection of the kinship-related morality by protesting against women's mistreatment and demanding that men should fulfil their duties as breadwinners. But she also demands changes in such central cultural institutions as the marriage system by advocating women's right to divorce and earn an income and the eradication of the dowry system.

The idea of women's protest and self-expression fits the local political realm, which entails a discourse on a ruler's morality to a certain extent. Tapati Kundu's political activity entailed helping poor people and settling disputes. She demanded help from the Block Development Office for people in need: clothes, wheat, paddy, and monetary assistance. She settled disputes by punishing the guilty party with a fine, just as informal village meetings may do. She says she always thought about women and discussed things separately from men with other women panchayat representatives, perceiving women's political action and interests as separate from men's. Her political action and thinking follow the local understanding of politics as the realm of kinship-related morality and patron-client relationships where women act separately from men.

Yet her own awakening paints a picture of village society as backward and unchanging: when she met the enlightened city women during the course she took, she realized how far behind she was. Awakening juxtaposes the backward village with developed regions like cities and foreign countries where equality reigns. Women's concerns are brought to the public debate—and the realm of awakening—through imaginary visions of the developed other.

Some of Tapati Kundu's aims are truly radical and difficult to pursue in the village. Although she says she advocates women's right to divorce and the eradication of the dowry system, she never worked towards these aims in Janta. She acknowledges the difficulty of putting any radical ideas into practice in the village and recommends that in practice women try to behave properly as far as they can and persuade their husbands to behave well. The success of women's committees depends largely on how their goals fit the local concept of politics. Local understanding of politics can help facilitate women's critical discourses, but also sets limits to action.

The local concept of politics explains how women's committees have been able to break through in rural and urban areas and among the high and low castes and classes. All female activists, including the Vishnupur activist I interviewed, share a concept of politics as the realm of morality dictated by kinship and patron-client relationships. This concept allows separate roles for women representing the high caste and class, and those from low caste and class: that of patrons for the former and clients protecting the formers' interests for the latter. However, despite such shared concerns as the need to help women in family disputes, there are crucial differences between how the urban and rural activists and high and low caste activists perceive their political goals as the following excerpts from female activists' interviews illustrate.

The distance between Janta and the city of Vishnupur is only 14 km, but the account that Tapati Sardar (a school teacher from Vishnupur and a member of the mahila samiti district council which plans the women's committees' agenda, both in the city and in the villages of the district) gave of the aims of the women's committee work, offers an example of how far apart they are socially:

> Our public work includes going from door-to-door to recruit members. That is our principal work. In addition, we try to solve women's problems, like that of harassment. We speak about government work.
>
> *What kind of work takes place in the villages?*
> When the prices rise we protest, for instance. We are for women's education. We help women who have been mistreated. We have to fulfil the allotted quota of newly recruited members before the district meeting. We have to go from door to door and convince women to become members.
>
> *What kind of change has taken place since 1972 when women's committees were founded?*
> In the beginning people did not understand our discussions. Now they understand and support us. There has been a lot of progress.
>
> *What are the main problems for women?*
> There is a big problem concerning unemployment. That is the main problem. There are many obstacles to women securing employment, in spite of which women have come forward to work

for their own interests. We have been able to make women understand that we can offer them opportunities *(sujog subidha)*.

Do you get involved in women's family problems?
Yes, we discuss that. If there is a problem between a husband and wife, or between generations of a family, they can tell us about the problem, and we try to solve it. We can suggest a solution that works only in certain places. For example, in Vishnupur a woman was burnt to death. We took the matter up with the police and the in-laws were arrested.

Is the work similar to that in the villages?
Yes. Our idea is the same. The organization is separate because of the distance.

What kind of change has there been in women's lives?
There has not been a very marked change in their lives. Earlier people did not understand why prices went up. We were able to increase people's awareness. There is some change.

Is there less family violence now?
Yes. The incidents of family violence have decreased. Occasionally, we hear of a husband or wife misbehaving. Sometimes the wife finds it impossible to live with the in-laws or the in-laws complain. We try to improve the situation. It is very difficult to get women involved because they have to take care of the household. We hope to arrange income-generating opportunities for women.

Tapati Sardar speaks as a representative of educated, urban women and her first priority is to get salaried jobs for women. Except for the well-educated and high caste ones, village women, most of whom are involved in agricultural production, are more interested in finding income-generating opportunities to complement income from farming rather than in acquiring jobs in service. Moreover, Tapati Sardar's account ignores the problems of day labourers. One of her main goals, protesting against price rise, is an issue that the urban and rural people experience differently. Whereas urban residents are inclined to protest against the rising prices of foodstuffs, the farmers' main concern is that the market price of their produce should cover the costs of pesticides, fertilizers and kerosene. Village women could not be mobilized to join the city women in their protest against an increase in the price of electricity because most of them have no electricity at home.

The agenda of Aparna Mukherjee (women's committee member from Udbastukendra village) covers the village women's issues in that she recognizes the need for creating income-generating opportunities for them and ensuring equal rates of payment for female and male labourers:

> This is not within the panchayat, it is the mahila samiti. Scheduled Caste and tribal women were trained to make shal-leaf plates here. In other units of the mahila samiti women collect milk from various houses and supply to the dairy. It is sometimes very hard to manage.
>
> *What do you consider to be rural women's main problems?*
> The main problem is that if women do not have a role in production, do not contribute to the household economy, they do not have any prestige *(marjada)*. On the other hand, those who earn a living have prestige. The middle class and middle castes have more problems. *Pon* (dowry) is another problem. But those who are able to earn to support the family, have a different kind of prestige.
>
> *Have you witnessed any change or development in women's lives?*
> Development has occurred during the Left Front rule. Labourers are earning more. Thanks to our movement, female and male labourers now receive equal pay for the same amount of work. Nowadays many women work in offices. More women leave their houses to provide tuition. They have an opportunity to earn an income. A husband and wife who work as labourers can both earn Rs.40 to 50 a day. Earning Rs.100 a day represents a lot of development in the family. They do not have to go without food.

> They do not have to manage with only one set of clothes. Previously women used to wear half a sari and save the other half for the future. Now women have at least two saris, petticoats and blouses. Earlier they did not wear shoes, now they do. That's the kind of development that has taken place.
>
> *What else should be done for women?*
> The main problem is that women are not educated. We now run a literacy campaign in West Bengal. The women who never went to school should at least learn to read and write a bit. If women were educated the whole environment would be different.
>
> *What do women gain from education?*
> If women go to school, they can get government jobs. Educated women know how to help their children with schoolwork. If the mother went to school, it is likely that the children would as well and the environment will improve. If low caste, tribal people and labourers were educated, they would realize that goats and cows should be kept separately from where children are fed. They will understand that one should not defecate near the house. Education creates awareness.

Aparna Mukherjee's theory about the prestige women achieve by having an income challenges the cultural code of conduct for high caste women, but not that of low caste women. Low caste women, most of who still struggle with the problems of earning enough to feed themselves, would disagree with her view about middle and upper caste women having more problems than the low caste women.

A low caste activist, Lakshi Bagdi, favours direct policy measures instead of consciousness building:

> We poor people have a [labourer's] union, while they are the rich people *(boro lok).* We poor people work for them under their command *(sason kore).* The more we work, the more the owners

profit. The union does not let the employers do whatever they want to.

Does the union take women's problems into consideration?
Yes. Although women still do not get the same payment as men in all the brick factories.

Do you go on strike every year?
Not every year, only if the owner does not agree to our terms.

Do you go on strike for any other reason?
Yes, if a female labourer faces problems, or has an argument with the factory manager, [or] if somebody insults a worker. For example, we take up our problems with work allocation and payments.

Do women find it inconvenient to attend meetings?
There is no inconvenience for them. Many women think that something bad will happen if they go to a meeting. There is nothing bad about the meetings that we attend. I think that going to meetings helps maintain our prestige *(sonman)*. We could not survive without the party. We poor people would not survive without the government.

What do you discuss in the mahila samiti meetings?
We discuss that we have to visit houses and make other women understand.

What do you have to make them understand?
We can explain that we have gained some power *(jor)*. There is power. If several women meet and move out, it is good.

Lakshi Bagdi was referred to me as a union leader, but she described herself as a union activist. Although she does not have a formal position in the union, she has been instrumental in mobilizing the village's female labourers. She also attended village women's committee meetings. Like the two Tili activists, she lived in her natal village. She separated from her husband almost immediately after she was married at the age of ten and returned to live with her mother.

I could have probed Lakshi Bagdi more about how she perceived women's issues, but it was clear that her heart was set on improving the living and working conditions of the day labourers. She perceived women's separate agenda as demanding equal pay for women and men in the brick factories. Like other low caste women whom I interviewed, she said that she likes the mahila samiti without elaborating on the benefits of the committee's agenda.

Although both high and low caste women participate in the women's committee, the aims of these committees are tilted towards the higher caste women's concerns. Social change (see Chapter 2) and the accompanying political turmoil (see Chapter 3) strengthened the diversification of the social interests among women. High caste and low caste women share an agenda to defend women in family disputes, prevent family violence and ensure women and children's welfare and education. However, such higher caste women's concerns as women's right to go out and earn, preferably from *chakri,* mean little to lower caste women, who enjoy a relatively unrestricted freedom of movement outside the home. Lower caste women are used to earning daily wages and managing their own income. In turn, some of the top concerns for lower caste women, such as their terms and conditions of work, are better addressed through the peasants' union (Krishak Sabha) and especially the brick workers' union (CITU). The peasants' union achieved one of the most significant gains for female workers: the implementation of equal pay for male and female agricultural labourers.

Trans-local political organizations have achieved the most visible forms of female political activism in rural Bengal. Outside ideas and organizations have had a profound impact on the village, but within the parameters set by local concepts. Political parties can employ women to take part in public protests because their idea of women as the protectors of society agrees with the village understanding of politics. Similarly, village women have welcomed the theory of consciousness building because it follows the understanding of politics as a moral discourse on the kinship-related code of conduct. The success of women's organizations in the village depends on their ability to build on the local concept of politics and provide an avenue for women's spontaneous political action.

On the one hand, female political agency is limited in that the women's committee is not called to resolve major village disputes, as the men's general meetings are. On the other hand, in contrast to the unofficial village meetings that often serve the interests of the important men in the village, the women's committee focuses on the questions most women find relevant. Since the Bengali concept of politics does not exclude the women's domain, women's political goals draw their agenda from everyday life. In turn, issues and arguments propagated through women's committees have a direct relevance to women's everyday life. For instance, many women pointed out how, once the mahila samiti started drawing public attention to family violence, incidents of violence decreased and became widely condemned in the village. Women's committees have also encouraged women not only to listen and obey, but also to express their opinions and arguments as the main prerequisite for their emancipation.

Nevertheless, the local concept of politics also constrains women's political action. The more in line women's demands are with the kinship-related code of conduct, the better they are heeded. This makes striving for radical changes more difficult than simply protecting the kinship ideals—but not impossible. Seeing women's agenda as separate from that of men helps women to identify their own agenda, but at the same time it may leave men and the larger society outside this agenda. Separate activism could lead to a situation where women are highly conscious of their needs in their separate organizations, but leave the authority to male-dominated families and public governing bodies. For example, despite their success and initiative in organizing women, the Left Front did not consider women as recipients of land rights in the land reform movement (Basu 1992). However, women activists do advocate the idea of women voicing their interests in their families and negotiating with men in disputes. Although parties, labour unions, and government bodies have often neglected women's interests, they have introduced a few successful policies: the peasants' union has introduced equal pay for women and male agricultural labourers, CPI(M) has organized rural women extensively and the Central Government introduced quotas for women representatives in panchayats. Women panchayat representatives do make the local administration more accessible for women.

In India, women's political participation has generally been identified as associated with kinship as female politicians are often considered proxies of their male family members. Together with the previous chapter, this chapter has illustrated that the role of kinship in female political participation is far more fundamental; it underlies both the concept of politics and women's political participation. Culturally conceived interrelated domains of kinship, gender, and politics do not merely limit women's political role and cause them to act as proxies, but enable and shape female political action and critical discourses.

FIVE

Gender, Kinship and Practice

A great part of women's activities, alternative discourses and subversive practices are not conceptualized as part of development, modernity, or politics. I wish to explore next the multiplicity of agency and how the different spheres of agency relate to one another. Do women's goals and daily practices differ from the ones propagated by the women's organizations? What is the relationship between women's personal goals and demands for broader changes in society?

THE REACH OF ORGANIZED ACTIVISM

The women's awakening propagated by women's organizations has indeed reached the two highest caste groups in the village (brahmins and Tilis). These women describe the desired course of development for women as the freedom and right to study, take up salaried jobs, move about freely and participate in politics:

> *What kind of change is necessary for women according to you?*
> Women should grow up studying and participate in politics. Women should participate in politics just like men do. That is what I want. Men and women are the same.
>
> *What kind of change have you seen in women's lives?*
> I want my daughter to study before getting married.

What other changes have you seen?
Much has changed. Earlier, women could not go out, they could not study. It would be regarded as dishonourable, but now women and men have the same rights. Previously wives could not move outside the house. Now if I tell my husband that I want to attend the mahila samiti meeting and talk with a group of women, and that we want to work together, he will allow me to go, but it was not like this before.

It is, of course, different these days. Women are not scared. Previously women were afraid of their mother-in-law and husband. Nowadays women are not afraid of anyone. Everything happens the way they want it to. Whatever they say happens.

What kinds of freedom do women have these days?
Women can arrange things as they want them. Previously they did not study much. Now they study and see the world outside and learn to figure out what to do. These days women have many desires (*shokh*): dress, education, and so on. Women have attained a new level in every respect. This is what we call modern. It was not like this earlier.

These depictions refer to a few pronounced changes that have occurred during the past decade: more women have received education, women have become visible in formal politics, and a few high caste women have taken up white-collar jobs.

As Figure 5.1 shows, the decline in illiteracy is most dramatic among the higher caste women in the age group 11-15 who have gained full literary. This is the highest rate among any age group and is also higher than the literacy of high caste boys in the same age group. High caste women have caught up with men in literacy and the younger age groups among low castes are catching up with the high castes, but the gap between the literacy levels of low and high castes still remains wide.

Women represent the village in the panchayat and women of all castes regularly attend the mahila samiti meetings. The first upper caste village girls (Tilis and brahmins) graduated from

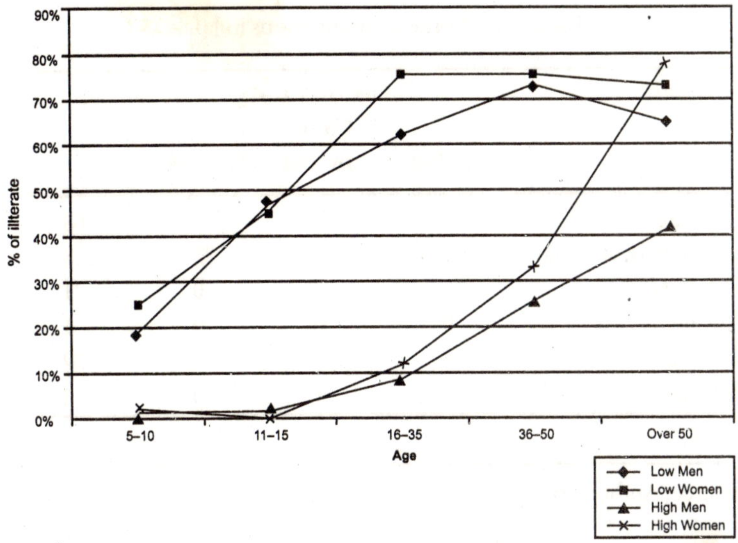

Figure 5.1. Illiteracy in Janta according to caste and gender
Source: Author's own survey, 2004.

college in the 1990s. Two of them found white-collar jobs (one as a teacher and the other in public administration). The general attitude towards women opting for white-collar jobs is favourable, 'I have seen that there is no inconvenience. I like service work. It does not harm one's health. A service job provides one with an income of one's own and allows one to buy what one wants. Without a job we have to ask our husbands for money' (a Tili woman).

The acceptance of female college students and women in white-collar jobs comes easily, even by men, as the majority of the villagers have little or no first-hand experience of such drastic changes. In fact, women's descriptions of sweeping changes appear contrary to the life that most village women lead. As Table 5.1 illustrates, the great majority of village women is not employed outside the home.

In general, high caste women do not work outside their house or move about alone outside their neighbourhood. While caste

Table 5.1. Women's occupations in Janta

By caste	(age over 15)			
		Caste		
	High (%)	Low (%)	Total (%)	
Labourer	0	3	9	68
Housework at home	94	55	87	673
Office work	0	0	0	1
Business	0	0	0	1
Student	5	1	4	32
Artisan	0	1	0	4
Total	625	155	779	

Source: Author's own survey, 2004.

dictates women's work to a great degree, the nature of woman's work is also a class issue. A Bauri (low caste) woman, married to a teacher, regrets that she can no longer work as a labourer and earn personal money because of her husband's position.

The gender division of work within different castes follows the metaphoric understanding of gender as portrayed in rituals in which the husband is alluded to as the cultivator sowing the seed and the wife as the earth bearing the fruit (Fruzzetti and Östör 1976: 121). When listing the types of work they had done, women sometimes assured me that despite the many tasks they performed and the heavy workloads they took on, they never touched the plough. Even the low caste women who work as day labourers in the paddy fields do not do any ploughing. In potter families, married women do not usually participate in the moulding of the clay. In the brick factories, where both low caste men and women work, men fill the brick moulds with earth while women carry the bricks and the earth.

Although Tili women do not work on the paddy fields or elsewhere outside the home, they have a substantial role in the agricultural production. Women are responsible for the time-consuming work of processing paddy into rice by boiling and drying the paddy seeds. In fact, the intensification of agriculture has doubled these women's work. Women also participate in the husking of the paddy. Vegetable fields are located nearer to the house than paddy fields, and Tili women from small and marginal farms can participate in all phases of vegetable cultivation, with the exception of ploughing. Brahmins as well as women from large farms, however, refrain from working in the vegetable fields.

Small and marginal farmers receive a great deal of their cash income by selling vegetables, but women do not see this money, since the sale of vegetables as well as the money are handled by men. If women want to buy something, they need to ask their husbands. Even women's saris are bought by men. Tili women can earn cash by preparing muri for sale both in and outside the village or by selling milk, provided their cows produce enough surplus milk. The income from selling muri can be substantial and is usually included in the family budget, whereas the sale of milk only fetches a negligible income that women may not necessarily make known to the rest of the family. Upper caste married women rarely move outside their own neighbourhood and village alone, although a Tili woman may travel alone to see a doctor, or visit her parental home if there is an emergency. They usually leave the village–to go shopping, to see a movie in Vishnupur and to visit their parents–with their husbands.

A married woman moving about on her own outside her home is under scrutiny as potentially it is a threat to the family honour. The higher the caste and class, the more restricted a woman's opportunities to go outside the house. Women going out alone are not immediately suspected of marital infidelity; but are seen as conveying a 'wrong attitude' of being carefree. Yet, most women do not live under constant surveillance and prohibitions. Family members usually share an understanding of the nuances of women's going out. Most women have the freedom to move about in their own caste neighbourhood, and are allowed to go outside the village accompanied by neighbours and in the presence of family men.

In contrast to the Tilis, the women of Bagdi neighbourhoods, who live close by, move about relatively freely. They visit relatives and temples outside the village on their own and go to *jatras* (plays) and the cinema without having to seek permission from male family members. Unlike the upper caste married women, low caste women can work as labourers in brick factories and paddy fields, transplanting, weeding and harvesting the paddy. They supplement their income from paid labour by fishing. Few Bagdi women continue the hereditary work of helping deliver babies at private homes and in hospitals. Other traditional income generating activities–which have become less common due to the increase of other work opportunities for Bagdi women–include tending cattle and collecting snails, dried twigs and manure. Bagdi women keep the money they earn for themselves and handle the household economy. Bagdi men usually hand their earnings over to the oldest woman of the household who is in charge of the expenses.

It is no wonder that the consciousness raising campaign run by women's organizations has had very little impact on Bagdi women: they have hardly any reason to campaign for free movement outside one's house or for women's right to work outside the home. When asked about women's problems, Bagdi women refer to the arduous nature of their work, poverty and not being able to educate their children. Since work is still mostly seasonal, more than half of the Bagdi children in the age group 10-15 need to supplement the family income by working (see Table 5.2.)

Bagdi women have, nevertheless, also participated in the mahila samiti. After all, as a group they are among the greatest recipients of the panchayat's economic benefits, and the mahila samiti was instrumental in bringing their needs and concerns to the panchayat's attention. The founder of the women's committee in Janta saw the upliftment of the poorest strata of the village as her main task, and one of the committee's main activities was to arrange literacy classes for women. Bagdi women say that a group of women working together brings strength, the samiti seeks to

Table 5.2. Children's occupations in Janta

(According to caste, age 10-15)		
Caste	High (%)	Low (%)
Farming	2	7
Labourer	0	35
Household work at home	0	7
Business	1	0
Student	94	43
Child at home	0	2
Artisan	2	0
Unknown	1	5
	100	100
Total	201	54

Source: Author's own survey, 2004.

solve people's problems and that the samiti loves women. One Bagdi woman noted that she never mentioned what happened at the meetings outside, thereby alluding to the subversive element of the women's samiti activities. Despite their many different interests, high and low caste women share an understanding of politics as the realm of kinship and patron-client-related morality, as inclusive of family life, and of the women's committee as being able to protect women's interests in family conflicts.

THE SUBTLE WAYS OF EMANCIPATION

The women's consciousness raising campaign has by no means been a complete success in Janta: its emancipatory goals are not a high priority for the low caste women, whereas the high caste women, who widely agree with the goals, do not seem to have been able to achieve them. Nevertheless, detailed accounts of the changes given by women illustrate that upper caste women have been involved in forging new identities in subtle ways. There is reform and reproduction, critical discourses and outright resistance. Some of these discourses are identified as part of *unnoti* (development), while others appear to be part of the eternal life of alternative discourses and internal conflicts in the village in the sense that they are seldom related to the discourses of development.

Married higher caste women may not have achieved the foremost goals propagated by the female activists and organizations, but they nevertheless perceive distinct changes in their lives when compared to that of their mothers. As mentioned earlier, younger high caste women are better educated than their mothers. Although child marriages have become rare, there has not been a drastic rise in the marriage age, as Tables 5.3 and 5.4 show.

Table 5.3 Women's marriage ages

Marriage age	Age			
	16-35	36-50	Over 50	Total
		%		
7-10	0	1	5	1
11-13	2	2	11	4
14-16	26	22	17	23
17-19	22	17	11	18
20-22	44	52	34	44
23-25	7	6	22	10
	379	161	174	714

Source: Author's own survey, 2004.

The average number of children has gone down steadily (see Table 5.5.). There was no significant difference in the number of children between the high and low caste women. The most common form of contraception by far is tubal litigation (female

Table 5.4 Women's average marriage ages in Janta

Age	Mean	N	Std. Deviation
16-35	19	385	3
36-50	19	166	3
Over 50	20	187	5
All	19	738	4

Source: Author's own survey, 2004.

Table 5.5 Average number of children in Janta

16-35	1.5
36-50	2.5
Over 50	3.9
All	1.7

Source: Author's own survey, 2004.

sterilization) which women usually opt for after having had two or three children.

Instead of radical changes, many women have experienced subtle reforms in family life to which the increase in the general standard of living has contributed. A higher standard of living, they say, enables one to be a good family person, live happily as part of a small family where women can express their opinions, concerns, and wishes. The goals of freedom translate into husbands being more attentive to their wives' wishes—taking them to the cinema, shopping and picnics. The introduction of phones in the villages has offered women a new, unobtrusive avenue to extend their contacts and space without moving out of their neighbourhoods. Although women are a minority when it comes to making calls (29 per cent of my survey), they, nevertheless, can make calls without general disapproval. Thanks to the phones, women are better connected with their natal families which, for most women, are a major source of support. Just a decade ago women could be facing food scarcity or were mistreated in their husband's house for years before the news reached their parents. Today the exchange of news is so intense that, for instance, news of loss caused by the hailstorm reached the women's parents within a few days, even if the women did not call their parents directly.

Due to the increasing prosperity, husbands are now better able to fulfil their wives' desires: women can dress better, eat better and decorate their houses. Most houses do not have much furniture, except for wooden cots in which the frame is strung with ropes to form the base. These days the trend, increasingly, is to do up the interiors: many of the wealthier houses are not only decorated by pictures but also painted and furnished with carved wooden beds, wardrobes, dressing tables.

DAUGHTERS AS THE VANGUARDS OF MODERNITY

Daughters are the vanguards of the local understanding of modernity. Tili women, who at the most have realized subtle changes in their own lives, express determination to provide more major changes for their daughters: better education, less hard work, new job options, marriage at a more mature age than before to well-chosen families.

> *Do you think your daughter's life will be different?*
> Yes. I want to make my daughter's life different.
>
> *How?*
> I did not study much. I want my daughter to study more. I want her to wear better clothes I have. I want her to eat better food than I do.
>
> I want my daughter to get a service job. I want her to work like a son. We are facing difficulties. My husband does not have much land, but I want to arrange tuition for both my son and daughter.
>
> *Would you like your daughter to work after marriage?*
> It depends on her fate: she may go to a good house where she is

> not allowed to work, or a labourer's house where she will have to work hard. But if I can pay a big dowry, I would be able to send her to a good house so that she would have to do only household work. If I cannot do that and have to send her to a poor house, she will have to work.

The most striking new freedoms are allowed for daughters. They are the ones able to move about relatively freely–not only in their own neighbourhood, but also outside the village. Unmarried girls are allowed to cycle, which married village women never do, and college girls travel to study in Vishnupur. The girls who were married in the village during my fieldwork were approximately fifteen-sixteen years old. However, most women, as the Tili women quoted below discloses, would like to see their daughters married at a later age, at approximately eighteen-twenty:

> *Why do you think that women should get married at the age of 18?*
> At that age girls are mature, they are aware when they enter the mother-in-law's house. I had children at an early age. I did not understand things then. I did everything as I was told to. I could not do anything in my own house.
>
> *At what age should girls get married?*
> I think girls should be married when they are older and have gained some understanding–when they have completed their education. If they are married at an early age and the family is poor, they will face discomfort. Also, they won't be happy taking care of their family *(sansar)* once they've had children. A girl should grow up, complete her education and then get married by the age of twenty or twenty-one.

Ideally, motherly love is expressed by ensuring that daughters go to school and do not have to work hard in their parents' house. The villagers are well aware of the fact that a college degree gives one the possibility to search for a white-collar job, although it does not guarantee one. Nevertheless, most are willing to invest in their daughters' education. One important motivation for educating daughters is the fact that affluent houses are known to demand educated brides. In fact, while checking out potential brides, one of the first things asked is how far the girl has studied. But education is also seen as a way of broadening women's understanding of the outside world:

> Women study a lot these days, but I am like a blind person. If I had studied, I would be able to see a lot more, do all kinds of work. I had a daughter and was widowed at an early age. My situation is that of a frog in a well (A widowed Tili woman).

Women say education enables them to arrange their own lives, to bring up and educate their children, to mix with people and move about. Illiterate women regret their inability to do financial calculations, read important documents, street signs and bus numbers.

In extending their daughters' freedoms, mothers are building on the dominant discourses and kinship constructs rather than introducing totally novel and subversive ideas. After all, a daughter's education is not perceived as a complete departure from dominant cultural practices, but a strategy to arrange one's daughter's marriage to a good family. Moreover, the unmarried women's code of conduct has not been as restricted as that of the married women.

Unmarried Tili women, for instance, are allowed to work in the paddy fields, which married Tili women never do. Among the Kumar (potters) women, only the unmarried ones are usually allowed to mould clay. Unmarried girls have easy and affectionate relationships with their parents and siblings. The same informality characterizes a woman's relationships at her mother's brother's house. A mother's sister is likened to one's own mother, whereas one's relationships with father's sisters are formal.

The different codes of conduct toward a woman's consanguineal and affinal relatives illustrate the difference in meanings. According to Fruzzetti and Östör (1992 [1982]), women in Bengali culture join their husband's line, while maintaining their father's blood, although they are unable to pass their father's blood to future generations. Women become members of their husband's line, but they do not undergo a complete transubstantiation. Fruzzetti and Östör define the meaning of blood *(rokta)* in Bengal as 'a category of substance that is permanent, enduring, transmitted through the male members of the line, the incoming women or wives of the line acting as its carrier' (1992 [1982]: 36).

Even though the cultural construction of gender and kinship contributes to the fluidity of the daughter's life stage, the village women who were first to go to college were true pioneers. They clearly crossed the limits of their conventional code of conduct and knowingly became subject to criticism and malicious gossip. The first girl from Janta who passed the Madhyamik examination initially studied against her father's and grandfather's will, earning her school fees by giving tuition. One of the village's first female college students, a brahmin girl, recalls her experience:

> Perhaps women can now move freely, but previously it was not possible. Now we can travel to the town from the village. It was easy for the town people, but when I stepped outside, people would say that I was shameless. For the townspeople of Vishnupur or Radhanagar it was easy to roam here and there, but when it came to us, villagers, people would gossip. If one received tuition from a young man, like I did, people criticized this and suspected that we had an immoral relationship. But now many girls take tuitions from him. I was the first one, so it became a big scandal [she uses the English word]. But now it is no longer a scandal. At least ten girls from the neighbourhood are taught by him.

The way in which the strong resistance towards girls stepping out of their homes to receive tuition and attend college has vanished in just a few years, is quite spectacular, especially considering the fact that the structure of housewives' lives has, to a great degree, remained intact. In fact, with women's age at the time of marriage having gone up and more girls getting educated, the gap between daughters' and wives' lives has widened. Many people now claim that the newly educated daughters-in-law are the main reason for family conflicts, 'These days they obtain a wife who brings Rs.50,000 as dowry and says: "I am not going to do your household work"', a Tili woman of the mother-in-law generation says. In turn, the young women and wives are vocally critical about their future position as housewives:

> Girls no longer want to stay inside the house. They say: 'Let us move outside and learn singing, or get service jobs.' This is what girls want. I think that if I had a job, I would go out. The outside world has changed, but nothing is happening here. (A married brahmin woman)
>
> *What kind of progress is needed for women?*
> The main thing is that men should listen to women, listen and understand what they want. Women should get married when they are a bit older—I want all this, some progress *(poriborton)*. We can go out only with our husbands. We have enough food and clothes, everything, but that is not all. I like to talk openly, I want to go out, but here I am restricted (a married brahmin woman).
>
> Women cannot step out. If we do, our husbands will be angry. In order to participate in the women's committee, we have to go out (a married Tili woman).
>
> There is no development for women here. They study and then go to stay in the in-laws' house. Women cannot progress *(unnoti kora)*. They have to depend on other people all their lives.
>
> *What kind of change is required?*
> If women who study could get jobs, that would be development. That way there would be development in the house and the village environment would change (an unmarried Tili woman).

As the above quotes and the incident that follows demonstrate, village women draw from the ideas propagated by the women's committees. My assistant, Asima (a married Tili woman), once came to my defence when the brothers of my host family demanded that I ought not to step beyond the neighbourhood for safety reasons. When the younger brother tried ignoring Asima's view of the situation, she replied, 'Do you think you do not have to listen to me because I am a woman?' She told the brothers my stay in the village was pointless if I wasn't allowed to step out of the house. If they insisted on having their way, she said, my logical move would be to go elsewhere and the brothers would end up losing the rent they received from me. The brothers could not argue with her reasoning, and Asima concluded the conversation by saying that she had more intelligence than the two brothers put together.

Women's committees do not only harbour these critical voices, but also offer such direct acts of resistance as women going out against the will of their in-laws to watch movies in the village video hall or television at their neighbour's house. But in comparison to my earlier research in a working class neighbourhood in Kolkata (Tenhunen 2003, 2006), covert acts of resistance, such as women sneaking out of the house, are rare in the village for the obvious reason: there is hardly any space that is unmonitored. In the former case, men stayed out of the neighbourhood for most part of the day and women could easily go out without having to provide an explanation. On the one hand, the urban heterogeneity, marked by its city streets and cinema halls, offer the freedom of anonymity and more opportunities for covert action and alternatives than rural areas do. On the other hand, with fewer opportunities for covert acts, village women are more vocal about their demands and rights than the urban women I encountered in my research area in Kolkata.

NO TO CHANGE

Not all women, however, are critical; some openly express their rejection of change. Some women are untouched by the discourses on women's awakening and unable to describe any changes, whereas others oppose the changes they encounter:

> There is a lot of freedom these days. People want it, but it is not possible for me to desire freedom. I do not desire it much because I do not think of myself as a very important person. I want to live the way my husband wants to keep me . . . I want my daughter's [future] husband to be educated and I don't want my daughter to have total freedom to do things as she wishes. What I actually want is this: I want my daughter to live according to the family's financial means. She should behave in a way that's proper for one living within a family. She should not act or behave in ways that other members of the family may dislike. My daughter should live the way my son-in-law would want her to—adapting herself to others (a married Tili woman).
>
> *What do you think women gain from studying?*
> Women from farming families do not benefit from studying. Educated women do not understand the affection of people in a poor house. We need very little education. We need only know how to sign a name (a married Tili woman).

For many women the act of defending women's traditional duties entails change because it is a novelty for them to be the ideal housewife, *gharer bou.* The rising prosperity has enabled some of the wives of labourers as well as those of small and marginal farmers to refrain from certain kinds of work. Farmers' wives do not have to sell puffed rice in the marketplace to supplement the family income. Instead of wanting to take up paid employment, most landless women and women from small farms perceive the possibility to refrain from heavy work as their foremost goal. A married Tili woman who says, 'If I were married into a service holder's house, I might not have needed to work,' summarizes the desired course of change for many women.

The rejection of changes takes place in different contexts and does not always simply imply the will to maintain the status quo.

Women themselves may experience their upholding of tradition as transformative because they feel they are protecting their status and honour. The above-cited defence of the conventional code of conduct is evoked by the discourses of change and development and therefore entails a reinterpretation of the dominant discourse. These women choose to reassert some aspects of the conventional code of conduct, leaving other facets of tradition tacitly understood and their portrayals of the conventional code of conduct may exaggerate the rigidity and homogeneity of tradition.

FAMILY FIGHTS *(JHOGRA)*

Besides the discourses I have so far looked at—how women perceive the desired course of change or continuity—there is another realm of power struggle in the village: the business of ordinary family life with its disagreements and quarrels *(jhogra)*. The latter, for the most part, are neither perceived as part of the local ideas of modernity and development, nor as politics. As the preceding chapters have illustrated, although political kinship draws on the idioms of kinship, it does not equal other forms of kinship; villagers do differentiate between mere party relatives and other types of relatives. Consequently, family and kinship conflicts in the village have the propensity to become politicized, but not all conflicts do so. Before seeking help and advice from the party, families first try to sort out things among themselves, seeking help from the party or women's committees only if the problem remains grave. In turn, parties and women's committees involve themselves in family conflicts if they appear severe and uncontrollable by the families as in divorce cases, men squandering their family fortunes by drinking and gambling, and men battering their wives.

Quarrels range from a scolding *(bakan deua)*, refusal to speak to someone *(kotha bole na)*, use of abusive language *(galagali)*, hitting, running away, threatening with suicide and even committing suicide. Conflicts may be short or last a whole day.

Watching quarrels and family fights *(jhogra dekha)* is a common form of entertainment in the village; the louder and more intense the fight, the larger the audience. According to women, a daily average of one incident provides the neighbourhood with a topic of discussion and commentary, thereby confirming the wisdom of a popular Bengali song according to which 'not a day passes without a quarrel' *(jhogra chara ektao din cholbe na).*

Quarrels do not only take place between household members, they also extend to neighbours *(para atmio*, relatives through space) and relatives living in other villages (in-laws and women's natal families). The biggest fights arise because of water and land disputes: location and sharing of wells as well as using others' land as paths. Quarrels between neighbours can also be about mutual transactions such as the borrowing and lending of farming equipment or money. Once a woman whose family bought electricity from the neighbour protested against what she considered an excessive price by first shouting at him and then cutting the electrical wiring, leaving several houses without electricity. Conflicts between neighbours usually start with abusive language (galagali), which may provoke hitting among the women, followed by a mutual refusal to speak to one another.

The most common cause of conflict with relatives living in other villages is disproportionate gift giving and the differing expectations between the receivers and givers of gifts. In one case, a pregnant woman's natal relatives, who had come to perform the rituals preceding the birth, left the village angrily after being criticized for contributing too little (food and gifts). On another occasion, a man offended his wealthy natal relatives by contributing extravagantly to a funeral ritual.

The weaponry used in family fights in a Bengali household is manifold and fights may result in subtle changes in the balance of authority within the families. The decision not to speak to some member or members of a household can be used regardless of one's position: younger family members can refuse to speak to older ones and vice versa. Instances of women hitting other women are not unheard of, but hitting is usually practised by those in the position of authority–elder brothers, fathers and mothers-in-law. Those in lesser positions take recourse to galagali, running away, threatening with suicide and even committing suicide. These weapons of the weak, to paraphrase Scott (1985), can be effective in bringing the desired results, whereas hitting may not necessarily have the desired effect. Trying to chastize younger sisters and brothers or one's children by applying corporal punishment is still fairly accepted, but beating wives or daughters-in-law is now widely condemned in the village. Moreover, the use of force may not subdue but feed the spirit of resistance.

Women described galagali to me as their way of defeating men. After some persuasion, they agreed to teach me a few expressions that they said might prove useful in warding off unwanted attention. This attention came mainly from the young men of the nearby town of Vishnupur who would approach me by saying 'hello', 'good morning' or even 'love is great' (this never happened in the village and rarely in Kolkata). While I agreed with the village women that the men were being rude, the phrases the women taught me were so obscene that I never had the courage to use them. After returning to Finland, I mentioned one of these expressions to a male friend, who had grown up in Bengal. Although I used the galagali just to demonstrate what the women taught me and not to offend him, he was dumbfounded–just as the village women said men are when they hear galagali.

Women may also resort to leaving their homes, provided they have somewhere to go, such as the house of their natal relatives or a friend's house. Running away may result in a divorce, but usually the husband and his family persuade the wife to return. A woman threatening to leave the house may succeed in drawing attention to her situation.

In order to successfully forbid their husbands from doing something, women sometimes threaten suicide, like a woman who forbade her husband to gamble, 'If you go there once more, you will return to find me hanging from a ceiling.' A Bauri woman who was unhappy in her in-laws' house persuaded her father to permit her to divorce by threatening that she would hang herself if she had to continue living with her in-laws.

Suicide threats work because they are considered real. I heard of three suicides in Janta in the last few decades–all because of forbidden love affairs. Two of the victims were young men and one a woman. During my stay in the village, there were two attempts at suicide: a young man consumed pesticide because of a land dispute and a woman told her family that she had taken pesticide after a fight over money. The woman was angry with her mother-in-law because she felt she was not getting her share of the income from their joint venture of preparing muri. In the heat of the argument, she hit her mother-in-law. On hearing of the incident, the husband hit his wife, whereupon she said that she had taken pesticide, a slow killer. While being rushed to hospital she confessed that she had not actually taken the poison. The family was, however, deeply shaken by the incident, and the wife may have been able to gain more say in family affairs by making them aware that suicide is indeed a possibility in desperate situations. Another woman had indeed taken pesticide after a dispute with her mother-in-law over whether her husband, who was not feeling well, should rest instead of going to work. The woman was rushed to the hospital and survived. Now she claims that she has her own way in the family and at times still threatens suicide to get things done.

My data on suicides is far too limited to draw any general conclusions, and I do not mean to imply that, as a rule, suicides in rural India are about making statements during family conflicts. More data might well reveal that suicide is related to such universal causes such as depression, loneliness, a lack of adequate counselling and/or a support system. My examples merely point out one context of village suicides: its use as an instrument of defending one's point and position in the conflicts of close-knit families. Even when presented as ways to persuade others, suicide threats take place in emotionally charged situations and women who actually attempt or commit suicide, are also underscoring their lack of alternatives. Women would not resort to such drastic methods if their opinions were heard and respected in ordinary family discussions.

Davis (1983), applying Turner's (1957) view on settling conflicts, examined family conflicts as a form of politics which aims to maintain dharma and tradition. According to Davis, conflicts occur when people protest against others crossing the limits of culturally appropriate behaviour. It is true that fights commonly occur when family members criticize one another for neglecting duties. However, fights usually stem from the fact that there are several interpretations of right conduct. Daughters-in-law may find their in-laws' criticism as unjust and argue for their view of the situation. Husbands may consider spending money as they please as their right, but wives may not accept this. Among the Tilis, men are usually in charge of the household economy, but women with substantial earnings–those making puffed rice or having a salaried job–often successfully defend their right to make decisions about their income.

The preceding chapters delineated the local domain of politics, while this chapter has introduced other interrelated spheres of agency: women's discourses of development and modernity as well as a myriad of subversive practices and alternative discourses which are not always associated with development or politics. The existence of various arenas of agency explains how women who reject modern ideals are able to gain wide authority in their families, whereas women who are openly in favour of women's new liberties, may not be able to introduce any of the changes they desire into their own lives.

The discrepancy between women's descriptions of changes and their daily practices is a good reminder of the importance of heeding both what people say and what they do. Moreover, this discrepancy is telling of the local interpretations of politics, modernity and development, as well as of the relationship between personal agency and that of broader discursive change. Not all women experience much incongruity between their descriptions of change and their daily lives because their understanding of politics and interpretations of modernity and development draw from the local symbolic system. They perceive development as a subtle reform of family life, a happy family life which entails better standards of living and in-laws who are attentive to women's wishes. Women participating in politics argue that going to meetings does not entail a loss of honour. Female political activists in turn advocate the protection of the kinship-related morality by protesting against women's mistreatment and demanding that men fulfil their duties as breadwinners. High caste women are motivated to take up income-earning opportunities that allow them to retain their honour and status, such as paid employment at home or white collar jobs.

MARRIAGE PRACTICES

Marriage practices are a central form of reproduction and change, and love relationships and love marriages cause conflict in the village. If family fights offer live drama in the village, gossip usually centres around love affairs. Young girls from the neighbourhood would drop in to chat and wanted me to know that the village had caught up with the growing regional trend of love marriages although, according to them, love marriages were even more common in other villages. It certainly is the villagers' perception that love marriages have become more common during recent years, although debates on and disputes over love relationships are no novelty in Bengal, as the Bengali cinema and novels written in the past decades show. Love marriages probably took place in the village in the past as well. The difference between the earlier generations and the new generation of unmarried boys and girls is that young people now proudly talk about their relationships, whereas no one appeared eager to speak about the love affairs of the past.

Love marriages are often understood, in both layman theories and in research,[1] as an indication of individualism and being in opposition to arranged marriages and tradition. The main flaw of the idea of modernizing love is that it presupposes a juxtaposition of the individual and society, and does not take the meaning of love and marriage in different social contexts and cultures into account. I suggest that love marriages can offer insights into the nature of social change, not as a clear-cut shift from tradition to modernity, but as to how cultures harbour subversive discourses. There certainly was an element of conscious rebellion in the liaisons that I saw in Janta, but as I will point out, there is no linear shift, no direct change from arranged marriages to love marriages. Arranged marriages are in fact making an increasing economic impact in the region. As I will illustrate, arranged marriages are not merely about reproduction of tradition but entail social dynamism and change. I will start by exploring the arranged marriages to which the meaning of love marriages is tied.

Marriage practices have not changed in the village, in the sense that most marriages are arranged and take place within castes. In present-day rural West Bengal, marriage rituals and their meanings follow Fruzzetti's description and analysis of the 1960s and 1970s' rituals, reflecting the Bengali construction of the person (1990). The gift of a virgin (*dan*) is the greatest and most auspicious gift a man can give, and this giving of a bride is accompanied by other gifts. The size of the dowry reflects the groom and the bride's parallel status, although the dowry's size is defined by many factors. Most women marry outside their native villages, and alliances are preferably sought from villages where a member of the extended kin can investigate the potential groom or bride. Similar to Fruzzetti's description of marriage practices in Vishnupur, there are no fixed patterns of exchanging women, although marriage alliances in Janta are often sought within the circle of one's in-laws. Nevertheless, the marriage circle of the West Bengali villages is more clearly delineated than in urban areas or in the refugee villages.

What has, however, changed drastically are the brides and marriage gifts. Fifty years ago the ideal bride was a child given to the groom's family, along with voluntary gifts of brass utensils and gold jewellery. Among the lower castes, instead of the bride's side paying dowry, *bor pon,* to the groom's side, the groom's side paid a *kanya pon,* bride price, the size of which was more customary than negotiated. Today the ideal bride is a high school graduate and the marriage arrangements always entail negotiations on the size of the dowry given to the groom's side. The groom's side lists the items on the basis of negotiations between the groom's and the bride's families and the parties agree on the delivery schedule. A large part of the dowry is usually paid in instalments after the marriage. The bride's extended kin and friends, tied to her family by a network of reciprocal obligations, often pool in their resources to raise the dowry.

In present-day rural West Bengal, the highest dowry demands are made by large landowners, especially those who also run small-scale businesses, and by government employees who, in the villages, are mostly teachers. Government employees usually come from landowning families as a large bribe is needed to acquire a government job. The highest strata of rural society can demand up to Rs.150,000–which a working class family, obviously, would not be able to afford. A labourer's or a marginal farmer's family barely earns the Rs.3000 a month that a family of four needs for basic expenses. Land is a crucial dowry measure for farmers. In 1999, when dowry demands had touched an all-time high, I was told that a groom's parents could demand a dowry of Rs.20,000 per bigha (0.33 acre) of their land. Since then farmers who do not run a side business have reduced their demands drastically due to low profits from paddy cultivation. Nevertheless, many landowners holding small and middle-size plots, especially families with more sons than daughters, have been able to increase their landholdings through marriages: land is often purchased with dowry payments, or given as part of a dowry.

Elderly villagers explain the onset of excessive dowry demands as caused by people becoming wealthier and wanting to secure better prospects for their daughters. Indeed, since India's independence, the intensification of agriculture and land reforms has led to new types of economic differentiation in rural India.

In Janta, dowry demands began in the 1950s, after the abolition of the zamindari system. At first, dowry demands *(dabi)* complemented and came with gifts *(dan)* given volitionally. According to Fruzzetti (1990), this was also the situation in Vishnupur in the 1960s and 1970s: dowry consisted of gifts, such as jewellery, utensils, and clothing, freely given to the bride who would take these with her to her in-laws' house. Villagers in present-day rural Bengal still differentiate between dan and dabi, but now they say that there is nothing but dabi *(dabir baire kichhu nei)*, demand: all gift items have become part of the negotiations.

The key dowry items, the brass utensils, were used for daily cooking until replaced by vessels made of cheaper materials, such as steel, aluminum and plastic, which replicate the designs of the brass utensils. The brass items, therefore, are no longer articles of everyday use, but are treated as valuables stored safely for most of the year, to be taken out occasionally, during some of the religious ceremonies. The higher the groom's status and position, the higher the number of the brass items given. Utensils and gold jewellery are not only part of dabi, but are also often exchanged for cash. Most women no longer had the dan they received at the time of marriage, as these were pawned, sold or given as gifts when their daughters got married.

The major change since cash was included as part of the dowry is that the groom and bride's various characteristics were given a monetary value. Elderly villagers claim that earlier one's complexion was not an issue in marriage negotiations, whereas today such personal characteristics directly influence the dowry's size. In present-day rural West Bengal, the bride's educational status, light complexion and holding a government job can reduce the dowry significantly. In turn, the parents of a well-off groom, preferably a landowner who also runs small-scale business and has a flawless reputation, can demand Rs.100,000. Parents usually try to find out about the potential bride or groom's character and reputation as any defect affects the dowry size. The wealthiest strata also consider the medical history of the potential bride and the groom, and blood tests are usually done to rule out hereditary illnesses. Most villagers explain these tests as being about finding out whether the couple's blood matches, interpreting the medical discourse through the indigenous construction of blood (*rokto*).

During one of my stays in Janta, a potential groom's family suddenly came to see one of the village girls, and the wedding was finalized and performed the same day. The groom was a middle-level landowner who demanded Rs.20,000 in cash, only about a fourth of what he could have asked. Later I heard that the dowry asked for was low as the groom had wanted to marry for love, but his parents forced him to enter into an arranged marriage. The bride's side was able to marry their daughter to a well-off family without having to pay a high dowry, but the villagers thought that by overlooking the groom's prior relationship, the family risked their daughter's happiness. Dowry-related crime in India gets much public attention, but I did not encounter any harassment of women for more dowry in Janta. The dowry system has rather led to speculations about marriageable qualities or the lack thereof in potential brides and grooms. Bride takers can prosper by accepting brides with defects and, in turn, bride givers can save by marrying their daughters to houses whose reputation is blemished. A marginal landowner family, for instance, knowingly chose a mentally unstable bride for their son in return for land. When the first daughter-in-law committed suicide due to her illness (she was not harassed by the in-laws), the parents wed their son to another mentally ill girl, receiving land once again.

There are many reasons why the practice of dowry continues despite its aberrations and the burden it places on a girl's parents. A dowry indicates a natal family's appreciation of a girl as well as her status in her marital home and village. Parents are ready to make economic sacrifices to see their daughters marrying into reputable and affluent houses. Moreover, the money given at marriages circulates. The bride givers may run into debt, but the bride takers become wealthier. Women consider a dowry as their share of their parents' assets that they leave behind at the time of marriage. Many small farms are only viable thanks to the wealth that the wife brought to the house in the form of land or cash that was used to buy land.

The giving of hefty dowries may have accentuated the Bengali construction of personhood and the meanings of kinship by raising the stakes between bride givers and takers: the exchange of wealth is based on expectations of establishing a proper kinship between the bride givers and takers. Rising dowry demands have, nevertheless, led to alternatives to the traditional marriage practices. Marriages are often arranged suddenly in order to bring down the cost of feeding the extended kin at the wedding party. These short-cut marriages are arranged at either the bride's or groom's home, or in a temple, which lowers the cost even further.

Such an instant marriage could affect adversely on family and kinship because holding a marriage ceremony in the presence of only a few family members could create a rift between them and the more extended kin. These short-cut marriages are often, but not always, love marriages. They have not drastically transformed the kinship system, although the villagers feel that marriages that do not follow village exogamy, influence the alliance structure.

The general trend of increasing dowry payments does not exclude diversity. In fact, the criteria in respect of dowry payments contribute to diversity. As a marriage broker emphasized, each case is different. Not everyone who could demand an exorbitant dowry does so, and not everyone who demands gets what is expected. In turn, girls' houses can decide whether they want to marry their daughter above their status, or whether to accept a house with a lower status, which will decrease the dowry. I was told that whereas service holders and owners of large landholdings continue to demand and get high dowries, landless and marginal farmers with small holdings and unemployed men are having trouble finding brides. Villagers claim that this as well as the lessening of dowry demands are due to the distorted gender ratio (see Figure 5.2). Indeed, there are significantly fewer girls than boys in the village which indicates neglect of female children. I did not find any evidence of villagers detecting the sex of the unborn child by using ultrasound technology. Usually couples who manage to have a male first born child stop having more children but this may not contribute to the gender imbalance as the ones who have girls try to have a son. The most likely reason for the gender imbalance is, therefore, that parents take better care of their sons than daughters. The skewed gender ratio may be doing more to alleviate the practice of dowry than its prohibition by law; dowry was prohibited in India in 1961.

Figure 5.2 Distorted gender ratio

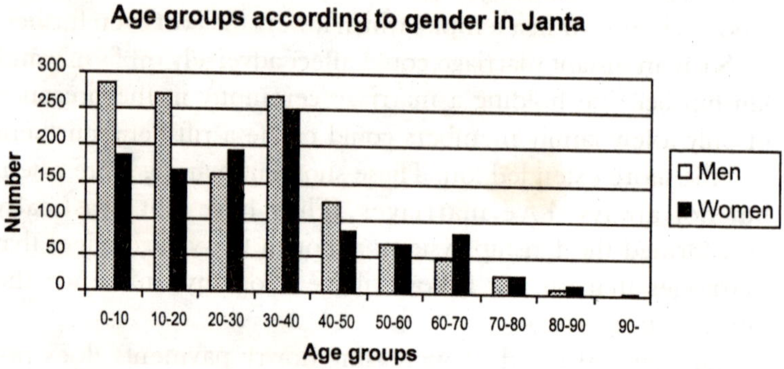

Source: Author's own survey, 2004.

THE LOGIC OF DEMAND

The spread of dowry demands (bor pon and dabi) has brought a certain type of market logic to marriage negotiations. Yet the payment of dowry also evades classification in Western or mere economic terms or functions. Dowry giving in Janta is not perceived as a compensation for the groom's family which has received an unproductive household member. On the contrary, often the need for female labour in the household necessitates arranging an early marriage for the son. As Chapter 4 illustrated, the intensification of agriculture, thanks to the adaptation of new irrigation technologies, has doubled the harvests and hence the need for female labour for refining the paddy.

In present-day India, the inheritance law is regarded as a major motivation for the prevalence of the dowry system. Since the law does not guarantee women's rights to inheritance by prohibiting the disinheritance of daughters, the dowry system is seen as a way of giving women a share of their natal property. However, these functional arguments do not explain why parents choose to give their daughters a dowry and not an inheritance. As an ample amount of previous research (Sharma 1984; Agarwal 1994; Madan 1975; Vatuk 1975; Parry 1979; and van der Veen 1972) illustrates, contrary to Tambiah's (1973) interpretation, dowry in India cannot be classified as women's pre-mortem inheritance, because brides have no control over most of the gifts that they receive at their marriage. Nevertheless, dowry gifts are considered women's assets. Contrary to the popular opinion that dowry denigrates women, most women feel that the dowry given at their marriage contributes to their positive self-image. As Oldenburg (2003: 9) points out, a dowry is a woman's safety net in a setting where women always marry outside their natal villages and where their rights in their natal homes lapse when they leave for their marital homes. Oldenburg stretches the argument to define dowry, rather controversially, as one of the few indigenous, woman-centred institutions in an overwhelmingly patriarchal and agrarian society.

Dowry is seen by villagers as a necessity to ensure their daughter's happiness *(meye sukhe thakar jonno).* Dowry is a form of collective property, and the woman's happiness is seen as depending on the fate of the collective family, for whom the dowry is given. Even the giving of dowry is often a collective act: dowry does not merely consist of the girl's parents' money/property but the extended kin and friends participate in raising the dowry. Although there is no guarantee what the groom's family will do with the dowry that they receive, girls' parents try to find out whether the potential groom would use the gifts productively (to extend cultivation or a small scale business) in the interest of the daughter's future *(meyer bhabishyot).* A girl's parents try to avoid grooms who may squander the money, or plan to use the money to repay existing loans, or on sisters' marriages. Giving land as dowry signifies most security for the bride, because land ownership is directly given to the bride. If the groom's family uses the money that they have received as a gift to buy land, this land stays with the married couple even when the joint family breaks up into nuclear units. However, giving land as dowry depends on the availability of land in the groom's village. It is not always possible to gift a piece of land that is conveniently located.

Although dowry demands in the Kolkata working class neighbourhood where I worked earlier (Tenhunen 2003) were lower than in rural West Bengal, women there wanted to give their daughters a dowry. These women received an income from paid employment and kept aside a large part of this to spend at their daughters' marriages. They wanted to concentrate their efforts on arranging their daughters' marriages with care and organizing attractive gifts, in contrast to their own marriages that were usually hastily arranged without proper gifts being exchanged. Women are not passive objects of marriage arrangements and exchanges, but see it as being in their interest to have a role in the process. Rather than trying to escape cultural and social constraints or pursue autonomy, women are pursuing their agency in shaping the cultural formations that constitute their identities.

It is usually the father's responsibility to look for suitable brides and grooms. Mothers cannot go to interview potential brides for their sons and most certainly not grooms for their daughters, but they nevertheless participate in marriage arrangements by finding out about suitable boys and grooms though their networks. The recent introduction of the working phone system to the region has increased women's role in marriage negotiations. After the father of a prospective bride had invited several mismatches to the house to see his daughter, some of the women living in the neighbourhood made a few phone calls and quickly arranged a meeting with a promising candidate: this potential groom owned some land, had a side business and was known to be good-natured and hardworking.

Rather than working towards stopping the practice altogether, the critical discourse on the dowry system has led to attempts to curb malpractice and reform marriage arrangements. In the village, women protect their right to regain the dowry in case of a divorce with the help of political parties and women's organizations. I was told that in case of the earlier generations girls were not consulted regarding the choice of their prospective grooms, but asking the girl's opinion has become a common practice now. Instances of the bride's kin cancelling the wedding and reporting the groom's party to the police for demanding additional dowry are not unheard of.

Women's interests have played a role in dowry demands, but it is the blending of gendered status and purity-related considerations that most directly influence the way dowry demands are assessed. Dowry negotiations are influenced by the supply and demand of certain characteristics related to hierarchical considerations. Dowry demands not only reflect class and economic status, but also factors that relate to caste considerations, such as education and a light complexion, which is considered essentially associated with upper caste, brahmin features. The introduction of the monetary gift has intensified the connections between different aspects of personhood facilitating multiple criteria for social standing and dynamism.

Much of the earlier research has interpreted pon as having to do with class and economic status in contrast to dan as having to do with ritual status. I argue that caste and class identities are separate and yet porous and they may interact. Moreover, the porousness of class and caste relates to what has happened to the different categories of gift. Instead of simply entailing adoption of an additional category of gifts to accompany other types of gifts, the gift of money along with the spread of the cash economy and the changing notions of property has led to the rearticulation of dan. According to Fruzzetti (1990), pon differed from other marriage gifts in that it was changeable and negotiable. In present-day rural Bengal, the logic of dabi pervades all gifts and facets of personhood. At the same time, the market logic of dabi is now based on hierarchical considerations.

To summarize, the gift of money does not merely represent class and economic identities. Rather, its introduction is connected to a reconstruction of gender and caste identities as well. I have demonstrated how the giving of money has influenced other categories of gifts, while the market logic has drawn from cultural considerations. Yet money is not the only agent in the process; gifts are essentially about constructing social and cultural identities: the interconnected domains of gender, kinship, caste and class. The introduction of the monetary gift enables one to make connections and set a price on different aspects of personhood, facilitating and intensifying the connections between different discourses on personhood. The rising dowry demands have intensified the meanings given to kinship; nevertheless, giving money as gifts also enables multiplicity, and I suggest that paying attention to the local variations of gift giving makes it possible to understand the ongoing creative re-articulations of tradition and the market. Several strategies are applied while bargaining over dowry and the excessive demands have led to options which might cut down the expenses. These include marriages arranged suddenly and attended only by the immediate kin as well as love marriages where, usually, the dowry amount would be lower than in arranged marriages.

PLACE OF LOVE IN CHANGE AND HIERARCHY

I mainly learnt about love marriages and relationships by chatting with the villagers, especially with the young girls. In addition, the interviews I conducted had to do with marriage as well as opinions on and experiences of love marriage. During my sojourn in the village, the neighbourhood was rife with the talk of an ongoing affair between a fourteen-year-old girl and her eighteen-year-old boyfriend who gave private tuition to children in the house where I lived. I also heard about love marriages that had occurred recently or in the recent past. Love marriages occur mainly among the educated Tili and brahmin youth who have less trouble with acceptance than the uneducated young people. The variation in the popularity and tolerance of love marriages reveals that love marriages do not merely reflect personal choice. Love becomes intertwined with hierarchies, and the popularity of love marriages among the educated youth makes love a vehicle of the new middle and upper class identity.[2]

Still, most boys and girls, even the educated ones, end up as farmers and farmers' wives. Younger brothers are expected to respect their father and older brothers' decisions, and young wives are supposed to show obedience to their mothers-in-law, husbands, and older brothers-in law. The shift from the freedom that women experience in their parents' house to restrictions in their in-laws' is not a new phenomenon and neither is the conflict between younger and older brothers. The critical attitudes of the youth have their roots in the kinship constructs, while the new prosperity and the rising level of education serve to consolidate the higher caste youth's rebellious position in a new social context.

Most of the men and women whom I talked to in Janta said they would accept it if their children wanted to choose their own spouses, provided the match was from the same caste. In reality, tolerance of love marriages was neither instant nor easily arrived at. It was felt that love marriages should be discouraged, at least initially. Yet many family members and bystanders lent silent support to these lovers, and love letters were exchanged through trusted people, sisters, brothers, and friends. When the couple's guardians discovered the relationship, they often beat the errant girl or boy in an effort to persuade them to end the relationship. The girls and boys triumphantly told me how they had suffered the beatings for not agreeing to marry anyone but the chosen one. The couple invariably succeeded in running away and having their marriage registered, whereupon the parents usually agreed to make it official, negotiated the time of the marriage ceremony and settled the dowry. The dowry would usually be considerably less than what one would have had to pay in an arranged marriage. Families in which love marriages have occurred tend to blur the difference between the marriage types. As a mother explained, her son had first entered into a love marriage, but after the parents heard about it, they arranged the marriage (that is, made it 'appear' to be an arranged marriage).

The differences between the two types of marriages are revealed in the nature of the marriage ceremonies. Arranged marriages call for proper marriage rituals *(anusthan)* in the homes of both the bride and the groom, whereas the ceremonies for love marriages can either be instant, conducted at a nearby temple, or a complete marriage ritual in both the bride and the groom's parents' homes. Love and sex are considered crucial elements of both arranged and love marriages. The idea of a marriage as the gift of a virgin links sex with marriage. If a married man is known to have had sex with an unmarried girl, he is expected to marry the girl as his second wife.

The general explanation given to the question why guardians do not usually approve of love marriages is that they want to have their daughters and sisters marry into families that are well-off. Yet, with dowry demands continuously increasing, it is doubtful whether marriages to more prosperous houses are always possible. Also love marriages upset the family hierarchy when a younger brother or sister intends marrying before their older siblings. The main objection, however, stemmed from one's desire to protect family honour. No father or older brother was willing to allow his daughter or sister to meet a boy before marriage, and certainly not in private, without guardians supervising the proceedings. If a boy is not willing to marry his girlfriend, arranging the girl's marriage to someone else might prove difficult and require a large dowry.

If guardians are unable to prevent a couple from meeting, they often want to rush them into marriage. A woman forced her sister-in-law's boyfriend to hasten his marriage plans by tricking the couple into a room and then forcibly locking them in. This not only put the girl's honour at risk, but the boy was indeed forced to agree to marry the girl as soon as possible, although his family had wanted to postpone the marriage until his older brother had married. Forcing the boy to marry did not increase the dowry demanded by the boy's family. He could not risk his reputation, although the forced love marriage was not to his liking.

In Janta, the acceptance of love marriages is facilitated by the fact that they support caste endogamy in the village and resemble arranged marriages in that the parents or guardians of the couples usually get to negotiate the dowry and set the marriage date. Nevertheless, love marriages may induce changes. The villagers speculated more on the changes in relationships with the in-laws than on the possible difference that this marriage could effect on the husband-wife relationship as opposed to that in an arranged marriage. Perhaps the husband-wife relationship was considered equally unpredictable in both types of marriages. On the one hand, love marriages are known to lead to divorces, while, on the other hand, arranged marriages are entered into with the expectation that these would lead to a loving relationship between spouses.

Most love marriages occur between people from the same village, and many married women consider it absurd that one's parents' house could be seen from one's in-laws'. A proper relationship between the houses would, according to women, require distance. They feel that a married woman adjusts better with her in-laws when there is a considerable distance between her parents' and marital home, because problems and conflicts that should be settled within the confines of a single house ought not to extend to any other house. Distance also helps sustain the meanings of kinship, thus upholding the honour between the houses. Even if in-laws have come to accept a love marriage, if their son-in-law lives next door, his visits do not become such momentous events as they would if he were to visit from further away. And if there is no proper meaning assigned to in-laws, that is, kutum, it could lead to kutums not fulfilling their obligations.

Women stated that the benefit of an arranged marriage was that the parents who arranged the marriage felt an obligation to see to their daughter's well being even after the marriage. Love marriages are therefore experienced as causing a change in the alliance patterns and the integration of families into networks of kinship.

As Fruzzetti points out, questions of honour and perceptions of love are at the core of the perceived difference between arranged and love marriages. Bengali Hindu marriage expresses devotional and physical love and the continuation of the kin group, *bongsho,* as its aim, but love marriages are perceived as expressions of mere physical love (Fruzzetti 1990 [1982]: 14). There is no denying that this anti-social meaning of love governs public discourses in Janta, and this explains the strong disapproval with which love relationships are regarded. However, the idea of romantic love also carries other meanings that are sustained in specific social contexts. The alternative meanings of love cropped up in what young girls considered as proper behaviour in love relationships, in other women's comments on love relationships and in women singing about love and longing.

The movie industry may also contribute to villagers' ideas of romantic love, but I doubt if it is such a one-way relationship as the villagers maintain. Like many villages in the region, Janta acquired a video hall a few years ago and villagers blamed the increase in love relationships on the cinema, especially on the daily video shows held in the village.

True love is considered as something final, and girls did not approve of having different boyfriends. Love is about one's own will, but it also appears as a force of destiny that ultimately does not leave alternatives. Even women whose marriages were arranged shared this view of love. They said that a girl who had once had a boyfriend but had to marry someone else could never be happy—there would never be *mil,* harmony and agreement, between the husband and wife. They called marrying someone other than the man one loves *du-numberi,* which means double-dealing. It is the idea of the finality of love that intensifies love affairs in the village and presents a contrast to switching partners and serial monogamy, common to many other cultures.

After telling me that college girls can move around quite freely and that many have boyfriends, a college-educated girl proudly added that they, despite their relationships, always maintain their honour *(somman)*. They are allowed to do anything with the boyfriend except have sex, she said. She went on to contrast the local girls' treasuring of one's honour with a Western woman's behaviour and what she perceives as 'open sex in the West'. Instances of pre-marital sex did happen occasionally in the village, but the girls, clearly, did not want to present their relationships as sex affairs, although it was the possibility of pre-marital sex that families worried about the most.

Three terms were used to refer to romantic love: the English word 'love', and the Bengali words *prem* and *bhalobasha*. Of these, love and prem have connotations of the scandalous meaning of love, while the word most commonly used, *bhalobasha,* also refers to non-romantic love between family members, conveys positive and accepted aspects of love. When women explain that it is best to marry a daughter to a boy whom she loves because she would not be happy with anyone else, they used the word *bhalobasha*.

The semantics of love are only partially reflected in spatial practices. Whereas all other social activities in the village have a legitimate place, couples cannot meet in the village. They can meet either on their way to school, or in the outskirts of the village where there are no houses or cultivation.

The first women's song I heard in the village was, to my surprise, about love and longing, which, as I later discovered, had to do with one of the themes of Tushu songs, sung mainly by Bagdi women. The singer, an old Bagdi woman, first ensured that there were no men around, especially, I think, no male kin. Like the tacit agreement that certain songs should only be sung in the presence of a single sex audience, there was also an understanding that issues of love, sex, and relationships between men and women could only be talked about in front of women.

Many of the women's jokes were also saved for women only.

This exclusiveness of certain topics creates the ground for alternative discourses, although the relations of deference are embedded in kinship categories. The villagers are aware of the alternative meanings of romantic love, which, along with the specific contexts and circles of people in which they are raised, explains the mystery of many people's silent approval and support of love affairs, although they could express their disapproval in other contexts.

The critical voices and alternative views raised and sustained among specific groups are not always communicated to other contexts, but can be raised in challenging ones. Love marriages in Janta are an example of how alternative meanings, such as the idea of romantic love, can travel from one social circle to a broader and a more public context. Raising subversive ideas publicly, like going through with a love marriage, is not achieved through withdrawal or an escape from the dominant ideas and discourses. It is achieved instead through reinterpretations, drawing from the dominant meaning's structures. The educated youth's growing tolerance of love marriages shows that the success of challenges and the interest in presenting them may largely depend on whether they are backed up by broader social change which is simultaneously induced by a variety of agents and institutions.

The preceding chapters delineated the local domain of politics, while this one has introduced other interrelated spheres of agency: women's discourses of development and modernity as well as a myriad range of subversive practices and alternative discourses which are not always associated with development or politics. The existence of various arenas of agency explains how women who reject modern ideals may be able to gain authority in their families.

As I illustrated, it is not possible to always recognize the sweeping changes women talk about in their daily lives. The discrepancy between women's descriptions of changes and their daily practices is a good reminder of the importance of heeding both what people say and what they do. Moreover, this discrepancy is telling of the local interpretations of politics, modernity and development, as well as of the relationship between personal agency and broader discursive change. Not all women experience much incongruity between their descriptions of change and their daily lives, because their understanding of politics and interpretations of modernity and development draw from the local symbolic system. They perceive development as a subtle reform of family life, a happy family life which entails better standards of living and in-laws who are attentive to women's wishes. Love relationships are associated with change and modernity; nevertheless they are also presented as honourable liaisons. Rather than emphasizing their individual freedom, young boys and girls depict love as a final force of destiny, emphasizing the chastity of these relationships. Women participating in politics argue that going to meetings does not entail a loss of honour. Female political activists in turn advocate the protection of kinship-related morality by protesting against women's mistreatment and demanding that men should fulfil their duties as breadwinners. High caste women are motivated to take up income-earning opportunities that allow them to retain their honour and status, such as paid employment at home or white collar work.

Yet, all goals of development and emancipation are not equally easily translated as part of the shared ideas of kinship-related morality. Dowry practices are at the core of the reconstruction of new social identities; consequently women activists' pleas to fight the evils of dowry by stopping the system have not caught on. Instead, women aim to reform the practice by curbing the malpractices.

Local interpretations of modernity and development are not complete departures from cultural practices and tradition, and change occurs also independent of the discourses on change and modernity. Although less heterogeneous than urban areas, village society offers opportunities for alternative discourses and subversive practices. The many forms of family conflicts show that the hierarchical structure of the family is under constant negotiation. Alternative discourses are even embedded in the relationships of deference, because they create exclusive circles that can harbour diversity of views. Actions striving from the motivation to reproduce the symbolic system can also be sources of critical discourses. For instance, young girls are educated and married at a later age in order to fulfil the demands of the bride takers. At the same time, the new-style upbringing of daughters can be a source of critical discourses: the new daughters-in-law are motivated to opt for more radical changes than their mothers were.

Notes

[1] See Gupta 1976; Simmons, vom Kolke and Shimizu 1986.

[2] Corwin (1977) speaks of a similar development in a small town in West Bengal. Love marriages and even inter-caste marriages among the educated youth were fairly well accepted in this town where a third of the inhabitants were immigrants from the surrounding rural area. Corwin argues that love marriages were accepted as they supported the class-like social ranking followed in the area.

Conclusion

I have been concerned with interpreting the relationship between local agency and broader organizations. At the same time, this book has described West Bengal's ruling party's strengths–and weaknesses–which haunt the party now more than ever. The state's forced land acquisitions, aimed at setting up industries, have tested the very limits of local agency and state rule in rural West Bengal. The village of Janta does not represent the entire state, but changes in the political affiliations in Janta offer some clues to the political conflicts in rural West Bengal.

Janta's CPI(M) leader aptly described the revolt of the opposition in Janta as a local Nandigram. As in Janta, the opposition elsewhere in the state criticizes the ruling party for its authoritarian style of government and its tactics of fear and force. My research supports the view that the ongoing conflicts in West Bengal have their roots in the fundamental weakness of the CPI(M) rule. The Left Front peasant leaders were able to mobilize the workers and the landless because they appeared to offer less authoritarian patronage than the old village heads or zamindars. Yet, the Left Front has not completely eradicated the coercive element from its patron-client relationships.

When the CPI(M) did not punish its local leader for committing a murder in Janta, the party's weakness was exposed. The majority of the villagers changed their political affiliation almost overnight. However, the CPI(M) has been able to rebuild its support base in Janta by activating its patronage to villagers. Whether one needs public health care, legal assistance, a job in new industries or in the government, one generally has to turn to the CPI(M) party in rural Bankura.

What inevitably makes the system based on bonds of local patronage fragile is the party's inability to extend scarce benefits to all equally. The Communist party's new slogan, 'Agriculture is our foundation and industries our future' is an unlikely prophecy for one of the main rice producing areas in India where the future is likely to depend on both industries and agriculture. Small and marginal farmers losing their livelihoods due to land acquisitions or pricing policies of agricultural produce are likely to increase opposition to the CPI(M). While the growing economic disparities may increase people's expectations of the party, it was those needing less patronage, the newly prosperous entrepreneurs, who led the revolt against the CPI(M) in Janta.

I found the villagers much less vocal about politics when I visited them in 2007 and 2008 than before–the party cadres' violent suppression of the opposition in Nandigram have made people fearful. Most villagers were aware of the atrocities, thanks to the media coverage of the conflicts, but preferred not to express their opinions openly.

As this book shows, the local concept of politics gives ground to a variety of interpretations and practices. It is the ruling party which has chosen to emphasize authoritarian patronage instead of providing social security through more transparent means of patronage. Intensification of translocal connections thanks to economic liberalization, large-scale social security programmes by the central state and improvements in communication systems may make it increasingly difficult for the CPI(M), or any other party, to base its rule mainly on personal patronage.

West Bengal's Left Front paved the way for the Congress party's victory in the Indian parliamentary elections in May 2009 by losing 26 of its 36 members of parliament. A sizeable number of voters voted against the Communist party in West Bengal in the panchayat elections in 2008, too, even though party cadres intimidated them from doing so in many districts. The Left still controls 13 of the 17 districts (two less than in 2003) but the opposition made significant gains even in areas where the CPI(M) was able to form the majority.

The opposition gained seats in the 2008 elections also in the Radhanagar Gram Panchayat to which Janta belongs with 16 other villages: four of the 12 representatives belong to Trinamul now in comparison to the earlier period of having just one. As in previous panchayats, the two representatives from Janta are from the CPI(M). The residents of Janta do not support the CPI(M) because they now view it as the best option, having forgotten the party's wrongdoings. They vote for the CPI(M) because of the resources and support they have received from it after the revolt. If the opposition's electoral gains continue in the state and the adjacent region, Janta may also choose to support the opposition when they judge it has become strong enough to protect them.

One of the CPI(M)'s perhaps often unacknowledged strengths is that it has organized rural women more efficiently than the opposition parties. I have presented an ethnography of women's political participation and agency, also exploring how the Left Front regime and the Indian state's reforms over the past few decades relate to the village social order and, especially, gender relationships. The research on women's politicized religion (Jeffrey and Basu 1998) and women's role in the nationalist movement (Sarkar 2001) has exemplified how women's political goals tend to draw from and reinforce the traditional code of conduct for women. This book has shown how local categories can bridge a way towards perceiving change and how global discourses facilitate local dialogue and resistance movements.

My analysis of the symbolic construction of village politics has not only led me to acknowledge women's role in politics, but also to understand the political processes as a whole and to analyse how politics relates to other forms of agency. I have examined how social and cultural categories are contested, interpreting interrelated realms of discourse and practice: politics, discourses on development and modernity as well as discourses and practices within the family and among villagers that are not always associated with politics, development or modernity. I will next sum up my ethnography and analysis, elaborating on their implications for the understanding of politics, power and agency.

INTERPRETING POLITICS

The party organization in rural Bankura presents itself as a hierarchical system, much like a family, and the top level of the local party organization is expected to act as a patron of its followers. Since most party leaders and activists come from wealthy families, politics entails 'little people' (*choto lok*) seeking help and patronage provided by important men ('big people', *boro lok*). The Left Front peasant leaders differ from the old village heads and zamindars although the coercive element has not completely disappeared.

Political discourse in the village parallels that of kinship morality, and the political parties' demand for justice means that the parties are expected to act in congruence with kinship ideals. Changes in political affiliation and fissures among party members have to do with serious insults and outright breaches of kinship solidarity between party members. Kinship is a metaphor for the party and its activities so that kinship-based party membership is differentiated from other types of relatives, defined on the basis of indigenous ideas of blood relations, code of conduct, sentiment, and according to spatial aspect. Although political relatives resemble other types of relatives in a moral sense, there are also crucial differences. Party membership is, after all, less arbitrary than kinship: one cannot select new blood relatives or kutum, relatives through marriage, as one can change one's political affiliation. Political kinship draws on the idioms of kinship, but does not equal other forms of kinship. Kinship and party membership overlap, creating conflicting solidarities. It is the overlap between party membership and kinship that allows parties to be efficient, but also makes politics a vulnerable and conflict-ridden business. National party organizations intervene and consolidate their power by expanding and aggravating local family disputes.

The political processes I have looked at have followed the classic morphological patterns portrayed by earlier political anthropology, both the functionalism and the faction approach.

As in the fission and fusion of the lineage mode (Evans-Pritchard 1940; Fortes 1945), a political conflict between two people in Janta involves their kinship ties, and the severing of a tie as a result of a dispute activates other ties of solidarity. The disputes in Janta bear a resemblance to factionalism (as analysed by Nicholas 1966; Bailey 1990) in that they divide villagers, who then seek patronage from different leaders. Faction is also the word that comes to mind when one tries to account for political incidents, as villagers themselves talk about politics in terms such as *bhag* and *daladali)* which appear to correspond to the words 'faction' and 'factionalism'.

However, both the faction and lineage approaches neglected the symbolism of local categories without which it is impossible to understand the domain of politics in Janta. It is the *symbolic* meanings of kinship and patron-client relationships that offer a framework of how the villagers perceive and practice politics: not only how groups of solidarity dissolve and form again, but also how villagers strive and fight for changes: which issues are self-evidently considered political and which ones get drawn into political debates.

GENDER IN POLITICS

Chapter 3 illustrated how the local concept of politics does not exclude kinship and the sphere of home. Family disputes, along with women's demands, are readily understood as political because politics in Bengal is not perceived as opposed to the women's domain of household and kinship as has been the case in societies where Western ideas of politics have evolved. Rajniti, politics, in Janta is the domain of the ruler's morality, guided by the interrelated meanings of gender, kinship, and patron-client relationships.

As in the organized movements of the past, women of Janta were employed by the party for their ability to defend the common good and not pursue their own goals. The village women themselves spoke in metaphors similar to those used by female revolutionaries of the nationalist movement to justify their action to protest the unjust deeds of the CPI(M): women came out to put out the fire. They did not leave their houses to challenge their cultural code of conduct, but did so as ideal women to defend the common good, the kinship-related code of conduct and morality.

The motivation of the local BJP in mobilizing women and the women's motivation for surrounding the police cars during an open conflict in the village both build on the idea of women as the embodiments and protectors of society, not that of the nation, but the village and the caste neighbourhood. Hence the village understanding of women's role in politics shares with the nationalist elite's solution to the women's question to challenge the British-proclaimed supremacy by insisting on protecting and strengthening the true Hindu identity and its repositories, women (Chatterjee 1993). Further research will perhaps determine to what degree the nationalist elite who after all had their roots in rural society were influenced by rural society and to what degree the village understanding of women's role in present day rural politics was forged by the nationalist movement and consequent political movements.

Women are allowed to play a political role as long as their agenda follows the local understanding of politics as the protection of kinship-related code of gendered conduct. The local concept of politics explains how women's committees have been able to break through in rural and urban areas and among the high and low castes and classes. Female activists I interviewed shared a concept of politics as the realm of morality dictated by kinship and the patron-client relationships. This concept allows a separate role for the high caste and class and low caste and class women: that of patron for the high caste/class women and that of client protecting her interests for the low caste/class women.

Political parties can employ women to take part in public protests because their idea of women as the protectors of society agrees with the village's understanding of politics. Similarly, village women have welcomed the theory of consciousness building (jagaron) because it follows the understanding of politics as a moral discourse on the kinship-related code of conduct.

On the one hand, female political agency is limited in that the mahila samiti is not called on to resolve major village disputes, as the men's general meetings are. On the other hand, in contrast to the unofficial village meetings that often serve the interests of the important men in the village, the women's committee focuses on the questions most women find relevant. Since the Bengali concept of politics does not exclude the women's domain, women's political goals as well as the issues and arguments propagated through women's committees draw their agenda from everyday life.

Nevertheless, the local concept of politics also constrains women's political action. The more in line women's demands are with the kinship-related code of conduct, the better they are heeded. This makes striving for radical changes more difficult than simply protecting the kinship ideals–but not impossible. Conceiving women's agenda as separate from that of men helps women to identify their own agenda, but at its worst, separate activism can lead to women being highly conscious of their needs in their separate organizations–leaving the authority to male-dominated families and public governing bodies. This problem has not gone unnoticed by the women activists interviewed in this book who regret that the decades of activism have not brought about drastic changes.

Chapter 4 discusses the impact of women's quotas in local governing organs (introduced in rural India in 1993) showing how this world's largest experiment in the decentralization of governance has indeed helped to overcome the problems of women's separate activism. As portrayed in Chapters 3 and 4, women still do not participate in the village's general meetings but thanks to panchayat reforms women have gained an entry to panchayat meetings and general village meetings called by the panchayat. Women's entry has not changed politics completely but it has shown the fluidity of the cultural code of conduct for women. Instead of appearing as mere proxies for the men of their families, women representatives are able to take up women's concerns in the governing organs.

POLITICS AND PRACTICE

Chapter 5 shifted the focus from women's formal political activism to women with no political background responding to change and development and the way their everyday agency relates to politics. As Chapter 5 illustrates, the campaign to make women aware has encouraged women's critical discourse and acts of direct resistance but has by no means been a complete success in Janta: the emancipatory goals are not a high priority for the low caste women, whereas the high caste women, who widely agree with the goals, do not seem to have been able to achieve them. However, detailed accounts of the changes given by women show that upper caste women have been involved in forging new identities in subtle ways. There is reform and reproduction, critical discourses and outright resistance. Some of these discourses are identified as part of unnoti (development), while others appear to be a part of the eternal life of alternative discourses and internal conflicts in the village in the sense that they are seldom related to the discourses of development.

Instead of radical changes, many women have experienced subtle reforms in family life to which the increase in the general standard of living has contributed. They describe a better life as the ability to be a good family person, who lives happily in a small family where women can express their opinions, concerns, and wishes. The goals of freedom translate into husbands being more attentive to women's wishes by accompanying their wives to the cinema, on shopping trips and to picnics at tourist sites. Thanks to the increasing prosperity, husbands are now better able to fulfil their wives' desires (shokhs): doing up the house, wearing better clothes and eating a greater variety of food.

Many women from poor households consider the ability to stay at home and not work as a desirable course of change. But my research materials do not give grounds to considering this as the sole trend among the upwardly mobile low castes because many of them also work actively to improve their terms of work. Moreover, treasuring being a housewife does not exclude the will to reform family life.

Besides politics and the discourses on development and consciousness building there is another realm of power struggle in the village: the business of ordinary family life with its disagreements and quarrels (jhogra). Quarrels range from a scolding (bakan deua), refusal to speak to someone (kotha bole na), use of abusive language (galagali), hitting, running away, threatening with suicide and even committing suicide. As Chapter 4 illustrates, although political kinship draws on the idioms of kinship, it does not equal other forms of kinship; villagers do differentiate between mere party relatives and other types of relatives. Consequently, family and kinship conflicts in the village have the propensity to become politicized, but not all conflicts do so. Before seeking help and advice from the party, families first try to sort things out among themselves, seeking help from the party, or from mahila samitis if the problem remains grave. In turn, parties and mahila samitis involve themselves in family conflicts if they appear severe and uncontrollable and the concerned families are unable to tackle these, as in divorce cases, men squandering their family fortunes by drinking and gambling, and battering their wives.

Davis (1983), applying Turner's (1957) view on settling conflicts, examined family conflicts as a form of politics which aims to maintain dharma and tradition. According to Davis, conflicts occur when people protest against others crossing the limits of culturally appropriate behaviour. It is true that fights commonly occur when family members criticize one another for neglecting duties. However, fights usually stem from the fact that there are several interpretations of the right conduct, and fights may result in slight shifts in what is generally considered as ideal behaviour.

If family fights offer live drama in the village, gossip usually centres on love affairs. Chapter 5 demonstrated love marriages as an example of how alternative meanings, such as the idea of romantic love, can travel from one social circle to a broader and a more public context. Raising subversive ideas publicly, like going through with a love marriage, is not achieved through withdrawal or an escape from the dominant ideas and discourses. It is achieved through reinterpretations, drawing from the dominant meaning structures.

The conventional forms of family conflicts are a form of agency that can be aptly categorized as resistance in the sense that they arise when people directly and knowingly resist the will of others at times, thus inducing changes. Nevertheless, my study also illustrates that the interplay of power relationships is not exhausted by the Gramscian concepts of domination and subordination. As Apfell-Marglin (1995: 86) points out, this view is based on the concept of an absolute boundary between the super-ordinate and subordinate, both bound in their personal identities. In addition, this view maintains the essentialist and ahistorical idea of the autonomous subject-agent as well as the absolute value based on it. My interpretation of the local concept of politics is in line with such studies as Apfell-Marglin (1995), Dumont (1970), Geertz (1980), Kapferer (1988), and Östör (1984) in showing how the concepts of dominance and subordination emerge from symbolic cosmologies, the super-ordinate and subordinate drawing from each other's identities.

As Chapter 5 shows, change occurs apart from discourses on change and modernity. Although less heterogeneous than urban areas, village society offers opportunities for alternative discourses and subversive practices. The many forms of family conflicts show that the hierarchical structure of the family is under constant negotiation. Alternative discourses are even embedded in the relationships of deference because they create exclusive circles that can harbour a diversity of views.

THE HETEROGENEOUS VILLAGE

My emphasis has been on how the increasing social multiplicity and the intensification of networks in rural West Bengal relate to cultural construction of politics, gender, caste, and ritual rather than on the reproduction of the shared tradition. Instead of a communal organ supervising caste purity, the tenets of caste discrimination are debated in various settings, producing heterogeneous interpretations which show in the increasing tolerance of transgressions and critical discourses. The quotas for the low castes and women in panchayats have decreased the power of village 'big men', at the same time shifting power to the party and panchayat officials outside the village. The dispersal of power outside the village is accentuated by the building of the mobile phone networks, thanks to which seeking help from outside the village during conflicts and crises has become easier. The 24-hour news channels expand conflicts by airing them out, while mobile technology helps political parties to organize protests efficiently. India's economic reforms have entailed an intensification of political protests and networks in India partly due to the liberalization of television broadcasting and the telesector.

Although both high and low caste women participate in the mahila samiti, the aims of these committees have been biased towards the higher caste women's concerns. Social change along with the accompanying political turmoil has strengthened the diversification of the social interests among women. High caste and low caste women share an agenda to defend women in family disputes, prevent family violence and ensure women's and children's welfare and education. However, such higher caste women's concerns as women's right to move outside the home and earn an income, preferably from *chakri* (in the service sector), mean little to lower caste women, who enjoy a relatively unrestricted freedom of movement outside the home. Lower caste women are used to earning an income through day labour and managing their own income. In turn, some of the top concerns for lower caste women, such as their terms and conditions of work, are better addressed through the peasants' union (Krishak Sabha) and especially the brick workers' union (CITU).

I have illustrated the rising dowry demands as one avenue for diversity in the village. Despite the pleas of political parties and women organizations to eradicate dowry, the system has grown over the past decades in the region. The oldest generation in Janta remember a time when no demands for money or other gifts were made during negotiating marriages, but since the 1950s huge dowry payments have become central financial transactions in the region. Several strategies are applied while bargaining over dowry, and excessive demands have led to alternatives which can cut down the expenses, such as marriages arranged suddenly in the presence of only the immediate kin as well as love marriages which generally require lower dowries than arranged marriages. The introduction of the monetary gift, dowry, in marriages has made it possible to make connections and set a price on different aspects of personhood, facilitating and intensifying the connections between different discourses on personhood. The rising dowry demands have expanded the meanings of kinship, at the same time enabling multiplicity.

The chapters of this book have shown how rather than the Western understandings of development and politics, it is the concepts of personhood which underlie and connect the local understandings of development, politics, women's participation in politics as well as women's everyday forms of resistance and agency. Political organizations have not put into practice their goal of the eradication of dowry because political work draws from and builds on the reconstructions of personhood, based on the marriage system.

Chapter 2 illustrated how development is perceived, practised and put on display as a bodily process concerning the essences of personhood and linked with other discourses on personhood. Development is conceptualized as part of the broader cultural standard of living, often captured by the expression khaua, makha, pora (eating, oiling one's skin and clothing). It is experienced both as a new emphasis on class identity and an increase in the collective pride in one's caste. As Schneider (1980) has argued, gender, class, and kinship connect through the concepts of personhood. Consequently, rather than doing away with other identities, improvements in any one of the statuses can contribute to other statuses by leading to the reinterpretation of all the interconnected statuses. Although acquiring a higher status by earning more does not influence one's purity and the ritual status, it can influence the collective pride in one's caste group. In turn, the new pride can motivate caste members to question the cultural code of conduct, based on the ideas of purity.

POWER

In broad terms, this study has been about power, culture, and agency and how to incorporate power issues into symbolic analysis. The apparent problem with analysing power relationships as a part of symbolically oriented analysis is that many general concepts of power are incompatible with the premise of symbolic analysis such as when power and politics are conceptualized as entailing certain domains of culture, politics, economy or the public sphere and when entailing power as individual autonomy, as if they were cross-cultural categories. Symbolic analysis does not provide justification for dividing culture into artificial blocks, that is, into culture as distinct from economy, politics or social relations along the Western categories of thought.

The main direction of the symbolically oriented studies, which assess power issues, has, more or less explicitly, been to adopt the Foucauldian understanding of power (Foucault 1980). The Foucauldian approach to power does not take Western ideas regarding the individual, culture, economy and politics for granted, but leads to an examination of them as discursive formations. Although Foucault focused precisely on the discursive construction of power, the Foucauldian perspective has inspired the kind of approach among anthropologists which would rather examine all social discourses as sites of power struggle than as the study of the diversity of power and political concepts. The understanding of power as knowledge and as the production of knowledge brings us close to the understanding of culture as power. Foucault does not juxtapose individuals and culture, although this juxtaposition is often evident when culture is equated with power, as with Bourdieu (1992) who describes culture as concealed domination and defines agency as individuals maximizing their self-interest.

The conceptualization of culture as power, as well as other concepts of power, poses a problem: how to avoid victimizing the subjects and account for human agency. The theorists of power have long noted the alternative meaning of power as a positive, enabling force; a definition elaborated on by both Giddens and Foucault. The equation of power with agency therefore offers a perspective from which to view the agency of actors who do not have authority. At the same time, as Wrong (1988: ix) notes, the equation draws attention away from the power disparities. The general definitions of power–such as power as knowledge, or structural, economic or individual power–fail to generate a general causal theory of power. They do, however, remain useful because they act as tools for critical analysis and readings, such as examining power as disparities in economic and social resources, which can offer valuable insights for policy formulation.

The meaning of power depends on the context of the argument and different concepts of power need not exclude one another. Examining local concepts of power, such as politics, offers a view of local critical faculties and agency, while the general concepts of power facilitate the examination of the outcomes and consequences of conflicting actions. In Janta, the local concept of politics gives ground to critical discourses. Politics is motivated by symbolic structures; yet 'big people' and 'small people' have been able to raise new and differing demands and interpretations of political goals.

The interest in practice and agency in anthropology (Ortner 1984 and 1989; Bourdieu 1977; Sahlins 1987 [1985]; de Certeau 1984; Hekman 1995; Kumar 1994; and Giddens 1994) has to a great degree excluded the sphere of politics as well as actors' capabilities to directly criticize the status quo. The predominant view analysing the domains of discourse, which draws from Marxist scholarship, has been to separate two forms of discourse: the active form of consciousness and the taken for granted form of consciousness.

Among anthropologists, Bourdieu and Comaraoff and Comaroff's formulations are examples of this line of thought. Bourdieu (1977: 164) calls the self-evident natural and social world as doxa: as distinct from the awareness and recognition of the possibility of different or antagonistic beliefs, which he calls heterodox. J. and J. Comaroff (1991) distinguish between hegemony, the taken for granted, the unspoken form of ideology and active and conscious ideology. At the same time they emphasize that although hegemony is naturalized, it is never total; on the contrary, they claim, it is always unstable and vulnerable. My study concurs with studies that perceive all social life as contested in that I found no domain as particularly static.

To sum up, this book has provided an answer to my initial question: how does social life entail reproduction and yet change is often forged in homes and away from public debates while personal experiences and everyday activities may also turn into politicized issues. On the one hand, change takes place outside the realm of discourses on development and modernity; on the other hand, local interpretations of modernity and development are not complete departures from tradition and everyday practices. Whereas many of the works on the symbolic construction of politics (such as Geertz 1980; Dumont 1970) have left the question of political agency open, I have explored how the local concept of politics can facilitate critical discourses. It is the symbolic connections and continuity between the local understandings of politics, discourses on development, and the myriad variety of subversive practices which allow personal issues and disputes, such as one's experiences of a child marriage or family violence, to be applied to the discussion on how society should be changed. Such notions as freedom, modernity and development are not applied in local disputes because of their universality or the supremacy of the Western model of modernization, but because these, through their local interpretations, offer concepts through which the taken-for-granted practices can be discussed and questioned. They are the means of awakening, of turning women's personal experiences into questions of social change, debated in broad circles.

References

Agarwal, Bina. 1994. *A Field of One's Own: Gender and Land Rights in South Asia.* Cambridge: Cambridge University Press.

Apffel-Marglin, Frédérique. 1995. Gender and the Unitary Self: Looking for the Subaltern in Coastal Orissa. *South Asia Research* 15, 1: 78-128.

Bailey, F. G. 1990 [1969]. *Stratagems and Spoils: A Social Anthropology of Politics.* Oxford: Blackwell.

Banerjee Abhijit, Pranab Bardhan, Kaushik Basu, Mrinal Datta Chaudhuri et al. 2002. Strategy for Economic Reform in West Bengal. *Economic and Political Weekly* (henceforth *EPW*) 37, 41: 4203-18.

Bandyopadhyay, D. 2003. Land Reforms and Agriculture: The West Bengal Experience. *EPW* 38, 9: 1-13.

Barth, Frederik. 1959. *Political Leadership among Swat Pathans.* Monograph on Social Anthropology, no. 19, London School of Economics.

Basu, Amrita. 1992. *Two Faces of Protest: Contrasting Modes of Women's Activism in India.* Berkeley: University of California Press.

—. 2002. Parliamentary Communism as a Historical Phenomenon: The CPI(M) in West Bengal in *Caste and Democratic Politics in India.* Delhi: Permanent Black: 167-208.

Basu, Dipankar. 2001. Political Economy of 'Middleness': Behind Violence in Rural West Bengal. *EPW* 36, 16: 1333-44.

Bayesh, Abdul. 1999. *Village Pay Phones and Poverty Reduction: Insights from a Grameen Bank Initiative in Bangladesh.* Bonn: Centre for Development Research.

Bhattacharyya, Dwaipayan. 1999. Politics of Middleness: The Changing Character of the Communist Party of India (Marxist) in Rural West

Bengal (1977-90). In Ben Rogaly, Barbara Hariss-White, and Sugata Bose, eds., *Sonar Bangla? Agricultural Growth and Agrarian Change in West Bengal and Bangladesh.* Delhi: Sage: 279-302.

Bourdieu, Pierre. 1992 [1980]. *The Logic of Practice.* Cambridge: Polity.

Bruns, B.G., L.Robert, and C.S. Chongchit Sripun Tiam-Tong, 1996. Village Telephones: Socioeconomic Impacts and Implications for Rural Futures. http://www.cm.ksc.co.th/bruns/rurtel.html. Census News letter No. 1 of 2001 : 6 August 2001 http://www.censusindia.net/results/eNewsletter_1.html

De Certeau, Michel. 1984. *The Practice of Everyday Life.* Berkeley: University of California Press.

Chatterjee, Partha. 1993. *The Nation and Its Fragments: Colonial and Postcolonial Histories.* Princeton: Princeton University Press.

Chaudhari, K. K. 1997. *Quit India Revolution: The Ethos of Its Central Direction.* Mumbai: Popular Prakashan.

Cohen, Abner 1974. *Two-Dimensional Man: An Essay on the Anthropology of Power and Symbolism in a Complex Society.* London: Routledge and Kegan Paul.

Cohn, Bernard S., and Gerald D. Berreman 1971. *India: Social Anthropology of a Civilization.* Englewood Cliffs, NJ: Prentice-Hall.

Collier, Jane Fishburne, and Sylvia Junko Yanagisako, eds. 1992 [1987]. *Gender and Kinship: Essays Toward a Unified Analysis.* Stanford: Stanford University Press.

Comaroff, Jean, and John Comaroff. 1991. *Of Revelation and Revolution: Christianity, Colonialism, and Consciousness in South Africa.* Chicago: University of Chicago Press.

Corwin, Lauren E. 1977. Caste, Class and Love-Marriage: Social Change in India. *Journal of Marriage and the Family* 39, 4: 823 - 831.

Coyle, Diana. ed. 2005. *Africa: The Impact of Mobile Phones.* Vodafone Policy Paper Series. Number 2. March http://www.vodafone.com/assets/files/en/AIMP_09032005.pdf

Dasgupta, Biplab. 1984. Agricultural Labour under Colonial, Semi-Capitalist and Capitalist Condition: A Case Study of West Bengal. *EPW* 19, 39: A129-A133+A136-A148.

Datta, Bishakha, ed. 2000 [1998]. *'And Who Will Make the Chapatis?': A*

Study of All-Women Panchayats in Maharashtra. Calcutta: Stree.

Davis, Marvin. 1983. *Rank and Rivalry: The Politics of Inequality in Rural West Bengal.* Cambridge: Cambridge University Press.

Derne, Steve. 2005. The (Limited) Effect of Cultural Globalization in India: Implications for Culture Theory. *Poetics* 33, 1: 33-47.

Dumont, Louis. 1970. *Homo Hierarchicus: An Essay on the Caste System.* Chicago: University of Chicago Press.

Economic and Political Weekly. 2003. Commentary. West Bengal: Untenable Umbrage. 38, 31.

Economic Political Weekly. 2002. Letter to the Editor. West Bengal: Schools out of Shape. 37, 43 (26 October).

Evans-Pritchard, E.E. 1940. *The Nuer: A Description of the Modes of Livelihood and Political Institutions of a Nilotic People*. Oxford: Clarendon.

Fernandes, Leela Margaret. 1994. The Gendered Worlds of Class and Community in India: The Politics of Organized Labor in the West Bengal Jute Mills. PhD diss., Department of Political Science,University of Chicago.

Forbes, Geraldine. *Women in Modern India*. Delhi: Foundation Books. 1999.

Fortes, M. 1945. *The Dynamics of Clanship among the Tallensi*. London: Oxford University Press.

Foucault, Michel. 1980 [1972]. *Power/Knowledge: Selected Interviews and other Writings 1972-1977*. New York: Pantheon.

Fruzzetti, Lina. 1990 [1982]. *The Gift of a Virgin: Women, Marriage, and Ritual in a Bengali Society*. Delhi: Oxford University Press

—. 2003. *Women, Orphans and Poverty: Social Movements and Ideologies of Work in India*. Quebec: World Heritage Press.

Fruzzetti, Lina and Östör, Akos. 1976. Seed and Earth: A Cultural Analysis of Kinship in a Bengali Town. *Contributions to Indian Sociology* 10, 1: 97-132.

—. 1992 [1982]. Bad Blood in Bengal. In Akos Östör and Lina Fruzzetti, eds., *Concepts of Person: Kinship, Caste, and Marriage in India*. Delhi: Oxford University Press: 31-55.

Fruzzetti, Lina and Perez, Rosa Maria. 2002. The Gender of the Nation:

Allegoric Femininity and Women's Status in Bengal and Goa. *Etnografica* 6: 41-58.

Gazdar, Haris, and Sengupta, Sunil. 1999. Agricultural Growth and Recent Trends in Well-Being in Rural West Bengal. In Ben Rogaly, Barbara Harriss-White, and Sugata Bose, eds., *Sonar Bangla? Agricultural Growth and Agrarian Change in West Bengal and Bangladesh.* Delhi: Sage: 60-91.

Geertz, Clifford. 1980. *Negara: The Theatre State in Nineteenth-Century Bali.* Princeton: Princeton University Press.

Ghosh, P.K., and Barbara Harriss-White. 2002. A Crisis in the Rice Economy. *Frontline* 19, 19: 14-27.

Giddens, Anthony. 1994 [1979]. *Central Problems in Social Theory: Action, Structure and Contradiction in Social Analysis.* Berkeley: University of California Press.

Gupta, Akhil. 1998. *Postcolonial Developments: Agriculture in the Making of Modern India.* Durham, NC: Duke University Press.

Gupta, Giri Raj. 1976. Love, Arranged Marriage and the Indian Social Structure. *Journal of Comparative Family Studies* 7, 1: 75-85.

Hansen, Thomas Blom. 1999. *The Saffron Wave: Democracy and Hindu Nationalism in Modern India.* Princeton: Princeton University Press.

Hardiman, David. 1999 [1982]. The Indian 'Faction': A Political Theory Examined. In Ranajit Guha, ed., *Subaltern Studies I: Writings on South Asian History and Society.* Delhi: Oxford University Press: 198-232.

Hekman, Susan. 1995. Subjects and Agents: The Question for Feminism. In Judith Kegan Gardiner, ed., *Provoking Agents: Gender and Agency in Theory and Practice.* Chicago: University of Illinois Press: 194-207.

Hill, Douglas. 2003. Policy, Politics and Chronic Poverty: The Experience of Bankura District, West Bengal. Paper, International Conference on Staying Poor: Chronic Poverty and Development Policy, IDPM, University of Manchester, 7-9 April.

Horst, Heather, and Daniel Miller. 2005. From Kinship to Link-up: Cell Phones and Social Networking in Jamaica. *Current Anthropology* 46, 5: 755-64.

Jeffrey, Patricia, and Amrita Basu, 1998. *Appropriating Gender: Women's Activism and Politicized Religion in South Asia.* London: Routledge.

Kapferer, Bruce. 1988. *Legends of People, Myths of State: Violence, Intolerance, and Political Culture in Sri Lanka and Australia.* Washington, D.C.: Smithsonian Institution Press.

Khanna, B. S. 1999. *Rural Local Government in India and South Asia.* Delhi: Deep & Deep.

Kohli, Atul. 1987. *The State and Poverty in India.* Cambridge: Cambridge University Press.

Kumar, Nita. 1994. Introduction in Nita Kumar, ed., *Women as Subjects.* Calcutta: Stree.

Kumar, Girish, and Buddhadeb Ghosh. 1996. *West Bengal Panchayat Elections 1993: A Study in Participation.* New Delhi: Institute of Social Sciences.

Lieten, G. K. 1992. *Continuity and Change in Rural West Bengal.* Delhi: Sage.

Loyola, Joseph. 2005. Inter-city Marketing Network for Women Micro-Entrepreneurs using Cell Phone: Social Capital Brings Eeconomic Development I4D. *Information for Development.* July. http://www.i4donline.net/feb05/intercity_full.asp

Madan, T.N.1975. Structural Implications of Marriage in North India: Wife-Givers and Wife-Takers among the Pandits of Kashmir. *Contributions to Indian Sociology* 9: 217-243.

Mallick, Ross. 1993. *Development Policy of a Communist Government: West Bengal since 1977.* New York: Cambridge University Press.

Mani, Lata. 1998. *Contentious Traditions: The Debate on Sati in Colonial India.* Berkeley: University of California Press.

Mencher, Joan. 1975. The Caste System Upside Down. *Current Anthropology* 15, 4: 469-93.

Mendelsohn, Oliver. 2002. The Transformation of Authority in Rural India. In Ghanshyam Shah, ed. *Caste and Democratic Politics in India.* Permanent Black: Delhi: 167-208.

Miller, D., and D. Slater. 2000. *The Internet: An Ethnographic Approach.* London: Berg.

Mukherjee, Soma. 2000. Cops Blame Parties for Organizing Lynchings. *Statesman.* 5.2.

Mukhopadhyay, Samir Kumar. 1994. *Permanent Settlement to Operation Barga.* Calcutta: Minerva.

Narain, Sunita. 2008. The Stink of India's Steel Frame. *Down to Earth* 15.7.

Nicholas, Ralph W. 1966. Segmentary Factional Politics. In M. J. Swartz, V.W. Turner, and Arthur Tuden, eds. *Political Anthropology.* Chicago: Aldine: 49-60.

—. 1996 [1968]. Structures of Politics in the Villages of Southern Asia. *In* Milton Singer and Bernard S. Cohn, eds., *Structure and Change in Indian Society.* Delhi: Rawat: 243-83.

Oldenburg, Veena Talwar. 2003. *Dowry Murder: The Imperial Origins of a Cultural Crime.* Delhi: Oxford University Press.

Ortner, Sherry B. 1984. Theory in Anthropology since the Sixties. *Comparative Studies in Society and History.* 26: 126-159.

—. 1989. *High Religion A Cultural and Political History of Sherpa Buddhism.* Princeton: Princeton University Press.

Östör, Akos. 1984. *Culture and Power: Legend, Ritual, Bazaar and Rebellion in a Bengali Society.* Delhi: Sage.

Parry, J. 1979. *Caste and Kinship in Kangra.* London: Routledge and Kegan Paul.

PRIA. 1999. *Women Leadership in Panchayati Raj Institutions: An Analysis of Six States.*

Rai, Manoj; Malini Nambiar, Sohini Paul et al., eds. 2001. *The State of Panchayats: A Participatory Perspective.* Delhi: Samskriti.

Rogaly, Ben, Barbara Harriss-White and Sugata Bose, eds. 1999. *Sonar Bangla? Agricultural Growth and Agrarian Change in West Bengal and Bangladesh.* Delhi: Sage.

Rogers, Susan Carol. 1975. Female Forms of Power and the Myth of Male Dominance: A Model of Female/Male Interaction in Peasant Society. *American Ethnologist* 2, 4: 727-54.

Rosaldo, Michelle Zimbalist, and Louise Lamphere, eds. 1974. *Women, Culture and Society.* Stanford: Stanford University Press.

Ruud, Arild Engelsen. 1994. Land and Power: The Marxist Conquest of Rural Bengal. *Modern Asian Studies* 28, 2: 357-80.

—. 2003. *Poetics of Village Politics: The Making of West Bengal's Rural Communism.* Delhi. Oxford University Press.

Sahlins, Marshall. 1987 [1985]. *Islands of History.* Chicago: University of Chicago Press.

Sarkar, Tanika. 2001. *Hindu Wife, Hindu Nation: Community, Religion, and Cultural Nationalism*. Bloomington: Indiana University Press.

Sen, Sunil. 1985. *The Working Women and Popular Movements in Bengal.* Calcutta: K.P. Bagchi.

Sen Choudhry, Sanghamitra. 1995. *Women and Politics: West Bengal a Case Study.* Calcutta: Minerva.

Schneider, David. 1980. *American Kinship: A Cultural Account.* Chicago: University of Chicago Press. 1980.

Simmons, Carolyn, H, Alexander vom Kolke, and Hideko Shimizu. 1986. Attitudes toward Romantic Love among American, German, and Japanese Students. *J Social Psychology* 126, 3: 327-36.

Scott, James. 1985. *Weapons of the Weak: Everyday Forms of Peasant Resistance.* Yale: Yale University Press.

Sharma, Ursula. 1984. Dowry in North India: Its Consequences for Women. In R. Hirschon, ed, *Women and Property: Women as Property.* London: Croom Helm. 62-74.

Strathern, Marilyn. 1988. *The Gender of the Gift: Problems with Women and Problems with Society in Melanesia.* Berkeley: University of California Press.

Swartz, Marc J., ed. 1969 [1968]. *Local-Level Politics.* Chicago: Aldine.

Swartz, Marc J., Victor W. Turner, and Arthur Tuden, eds. 1966. Introduction, *Political Anthropology.* Chicago: Aldine.

Telegraph. 2000. Trinamul, CPM in nightlong bloodbath. 21 May.

Tambiah, Stanley. 1973. Dowry and Bridewealth and the Property Rights of Women. In Jack Goody and Stanley J. Tambiah, eds. *Bridewealth and Dowry.* London: Cambridge University Press: 61-98.

Tenhunen Sirpa. 2003. *Secret Freedom in the City: Women's Wage Work and Agency in Calcutta.* Quebec: World Heritage Press.

—. 2006. Transforming Boundaries: Women's Work and Domesticity in Calcutta. In Lina Fruzzetti and Sirpa Tenhunen, eds. *Culture, Power and Agency: Gender in Indian Ethnography.* Stree. Kolkata: 110-34.

—. 2008. Mobile Technology in the Village: ICTs, Culture, and Social Logistics in India. *Journal of the Royal Anthropological Institute* 14, 3 (September): 515-34.

Times of India. 2004. Political Murders Highest in Bengal: Pranab (16 April). http://timesofindia.indiatimes.com/cms.dll/xml/uncomp/

articleshow?msid=619543

Turner, Victor W. 1957. *Schism and Continuity in an African Society.* Manchester: Manchester University Press.

Van der Veen, Klas. 1972. *I Give Thee My Daughter - A Study of Marriage and Hierarchy Among the Anavil Brahmins of South Gujarat.* Assen: Van Gorcum.

Vatuk, Sylvia. 1975. Gifts and Affines in North India. *Contributions to Indian Sociology* 9, 2: 155-96.

Williams, G. 1999. Panchayati Raj and the Changing Micro-politics of West Bengal. In Ben Rogaly, Harriss-White and Sugata Bose, eds. *Sonar Bangla? Agricultural Growth and Agrarian Change in West Bengal and Bangladesh.* Delhi: Sage: 229-52.

Wolpert, Stanley. 1989 [1977]. *A New History of India.* New York: Oxford University Press.

Wrong, Dennis. 1988 [1979] *Power: Its Forms, Bases, and Uses.* Oxford: Blackwell.

Yanagisako, Sylvia Junko. 1979. Family and Household: The Analysis of Domestic Groups. *Annual Review of Anthropology* 8: 161-205.

Index